"Page after liberating page made my heart cry out 'FREEDOM!!!' We are translating this book into Asian languages as quickly as possible so we can equip thousands of leaders to become channels of God's Brilliant Plan to their people." **Jim Harris, President, Relevant Expeditions**

"Mark Drake is a true 'voice' in the Body of Christ, not just an echo repeating what others are saying. The result...lives and churches are being changed." **Bill Matthews, Pastor**

"Mark's teaching on the power and presence of the Holy Spirit is the best I have ever heard." **Micah Smith, Pastor, Missionary, Author**

"The power of Mark's teaching on 'Christ living in and through us'...I have never heard anything like it." **Jim Keyes, Pastor, Missionary, Professor**

"This is a ministry of high integrity, unrelenting transparency, miraculous anointing, heart-healing teaching and deep love for the local church. I know of no other quite like it." **Fred Mcglone, Pastor**

"Three things characterize the ministry of Mark Drake- an authentic move of God, genuinely changed lives and unquestionable integrity." **Tom Goetz, Pastor**

"Our whole approach towards ministry has been affected because of Mark's message about the transforming power of God's Grace as the 'unearned life of Jesus living through us'." **JR Markle, Pastor**

"Mark certainly has a powerful anointing but he also has a teaching gift that is causing genuine, lasting change in people's lives." **Ronnie Holmes, Pastor**

"Mark's ministry has completely changed my life and my church. God is moving in ways we never dreamed and we are very grateful!" **Gary Plaugher, Pastor**

"The significance and scope of the change from the Old to the New Covenants is one of the least understood matters in the Church. In a warm and engaging style, Mark Drake highlights the importance of...living in the reality of this shift." **Dr. Stephen R. Crosby, Professor, Pastor, Author**

Copyright ©2008 by Mark Drake
markdrake@aol.com
markdrakeministries.com

Cover design by Henry Hoffarth, Creative Vision Design
www.creativevisiondesigncvd.com

Book layout by Joseph B. Geddes, Geddes Technology Consulting
joe@geddestech.com

Editorial work by Lori K. Jones

Printing provided by Creative Vision Design
www.creativevisiondesigncvd.com

Back Cover Photo by Shalem Mathew
www.shalemphotography.com

First printing edition, 2008
Reprinted 2011
ISBN 978-0-9843433-0-0

Dedication

This book exists because my wife refused to stop loving me.
During the worst five years of my life I directed many of my
fears, frustrations and anger towards her. But she refused to stop
loving me, she refused to stop forgiving me, and she refused to
stop believing in me.

For nearly four decades I have given her many reasons to choose
a different lifestyle and a different person to live it with.
But she has continued to choose me.

Linda, this one's for you.

I am also indebted to a small group of fellow-searchers who have
allowed me to ask far more questions than I've had answers
for…and continue to lovingly allow me to pretend to be one of
their leaders:
my spiritual family in Covenant Family Church, St. Louis, MO.

Mark Drake,
June 2008

The Search

1– Easy and Light? You're Kidding!

2– Now I'm Talking To Myself

3– Is It This or Is It That?

4– No, It's Not That…or That…or That

5– It's About Power…I Think

6– It Can't Be Me, So It Must Be Him

7– What Is the New Covenant, Really?

8– On, In…What's The Big Deal?

9– Whose Fruit Is This, Anyway?

10– The Law Was Meant To Fail

11– Threats or Promises? I Am So Confused

12– I Think I Know What…But How?

13– Relieved To Be Just A Lump of Clay

14– Who Is Doing The Work Here?

15– The "Do-It- Yourself" Dilemma

16– The "Do-It- To- Me" Solution

17– Please Do Something To Me

18– But Surely I Have To Do Something

19– Take Your Medicine

20– Stop Pretending

21– I Am So Mad At Myself!

22– Interact With The True Transformer

23– Rewire The Way I Think

24– Tying Up Loose Ends

God's Brilliant Plan

*...searching for the Easy and Light life
Jesus promised*

Chapter One

Easy and Light? You're Kidding!

Something was wrong; something was very wrong.

After over twenty-five years of success in both ministry and business, I was now experiencing external failure and internal meltdown. The foundation of everything I believed about myself and about God was being shaken, and I was in the middle of the most painful, embarrassing season of my life. And no amount of prayer and fasting could stop it.

For years, I was viewed by most who knew me as a godly man who had life pretty much under control. I was a good advertisement for the *"attractive gospel"*. I was a walking billboard that advertised how good the Christian life could be: happy family, prosperous ministry, top-notch business and lots of smiling faces. But in 1992, a snowball effect of circumstances began to overtake me and the *faith platitudes* and *charismatic clichés* I had been trusting in turned out to be just that; platitudes and clichés. I am not referring to anyone else's faulty foundation, just mine.

A Perfect Storm Of Circumstances

By early 1992, my best friend and senior pastor had left his wife and family, and walked away from the values and commitments to which we had both pledged our lives for many years. The disappointment was so deep and painful within me I felt that I had to turn my position over to other leaders, and my wife and I decided to step away from ministry and take some time off. We had been pastoring our entire adult lives and needed a break.

We had also been building a leadership consulting business that in ten years had gone from operating out of a garage to being listed as the largest of its kind in the world. So, at least we knew we could support ourselves during our short hiatus. Little did we suspect this short break would turn into the worst five years of our lives.

Just months after relocating to another state, the business began falling apart. The things that had grown the business so successfully for the past ten years now seemed to be killing it. Three of our key people defrauded and embezzled large amounts of money from our offices. We had hired these people because they were Christians and we felt they had the values needed for us to build a strong, moral company together. We were wrong.

In 1993, the worst flood ever recorded hit the Midwest and none of our losses were covered by insurance. Praying and believing that the flood waters would recede soon and the business would rebound, we felt that integrity demanded, and our confession of faith required, that we continue paying our employees. To do anything less would be a sign of unbelief. Nine months later the waters did recede and life returned to normal...except we had liquidated every asset and used up all our retirement funds. And we still lost all but one employee. Our business was gutted, our retirement was gone and our credit was destroyed. And no matter how much we prayed, things just got worse. I had never feared that God might not take care of me and my family, but I began to wonder now.

That same year, my wife's mother, who had been in excellent health, died in the back seat of the car while being driven to the doctor for what we thought was a minor respiratory infection. Three months later, we drove down to Branson, MO, to visit my side of the family and get some much needed, *and free*, rest. Early the next morning I arranged to take my uncle fishing, but he started to feel strange and died of a heart attack on the way to the hospital. Just a few days later, my forty-year old sister died of cancer, leaving a husband and two young teenage children. We were very close and it was very hard.

By the end of 1993, we were seriously struggling to understand what we could possibly be doing wrong that would cause God to allow such devastation to fall into our lives. We repented of everything we could think of and *confessed the Word* until we were hoarse. I thought I had hit bottom when the parents of our son's new bride had to pay to rent my tuxedo so no one would be embarrassed by me at the wedding. I was wrong. That was not the bottom.

In 1994, an outpouring of the Spirit began in the *"mega-church"* we were a part of and I started to believe all the trials of the past two years had been designed to prepare me for a true visitation from God. I was wrong. For the next three years, thousands of people came from around the country because of the amazing things God was doing in our church for seemingly everyone...but me! I got in every prayer line and received prayer from every notable minister that came through. I cried, I confessed and I finally stooped to doing a *"courtesy drop"* in the prayer line.

(For non-charismatics, that means I fell down when I was prayed for because everyone else did.) I received several prophetic words from reliable people that our situation was going to turn around. But instead of getting better, things got worse. I could not find the presence of God anywhere. I prayed more, read my Bible more and went to more meetings than ever in my life; and felt more empty and alone than ever in my life.

After five long years, I had to admit all the things that had produced such enviable fruit in my life for so many years had now stopped working; and I couldn't do anything to change the downward slide. I was still a Christian. I still believed in my eternal salvation through Christ. I was not living in rebellious sin that I knew of. But I felt trapped, terrified and spiritually abandoned. I felt rejected and completely unloved by God. Life had become unbearable and I was an empty shell.

For most of 1996, my wife was seriously worried that one day I wouldn't come home; that I would just disappear. It was the only time in my life that the thought of suicide held some small attraction. This book is dedicated to her because she refused to stop loving and forgiving me during those dark days.

Driven To Search

The good news is that this seemingly out-of-control ride became the catalyst for the greatest discovery of my Christian life and it drove me into an all consuming search to find the *"easy and light"* life Jesus promised in Matt. 11:30.

No matter how many translations I read, this passage still comes out the same. Jesus boldly proclaims:

> *"All of you who have been worn out and worn down from trying so hard to be what you think God wants you to be and do what you think God wants you to do, come to me and I will give you rest. Come and learn my way of living life. I have a life to give*

you that will be easy and light. It will fit you perfectly; it will rest on your shoulders like it was tailor-made for you. My yoke upon you will be <u>easy</u> and the burden I lay on you will be <u>light</u> because I will carry the load as you learn to walk along with me."

Now, after all my years as an *"expert,"* I had to admit I just didn't understand what Jesus was talking about. After many years of apparent success, my inability to now make life *"work,"* and the utter confusion my inability brought me, became the most humiliating experience I have ever had. And, for five long, embarrassing, gut-wrenching years it just got worse. And then came January, 1997, when the years of struggle abruptly changed and a new search began: my personal, passionate search for the *"Easy and Light Life"* Jesus promised.

Inexplicable Encounter

We all have major mile-markers in our personal lives: graduation, marriage, that first job, the birth of child, the death of a spouse, etc. Like most believers, my life can be divided by the time I lived before being born again, pre-April 1967, and after my new birth in Christ. But my personal journey can further be divided into *"before January 1997 and after January 1997."* The five years of intense frustration leading up to January 1997 culminated in a nearly complete spiritual collapse. By New Year's Eve of 1996, that collapse resulted in finally giving up any hope of ever again experiencing the presence of God, or feeling any sense of divine acceptance and fulfillment.

And then, at about 10:15 pm, on January 16, 1997, the Holy Spirit fell upon me in a way I cannot even come close to explaining. But I know it was genuine. That night I began seventeen days of inexplicable, intensely personal encounters with God.

For much of the time during that two and a half week period, I was unaware of my surroundings and often unaware of myself, but I was extremely aware of the nearness of God. I frequently couldn't work, drive, or, at times, even speak English. My wife had to take care of me, our home, our family, and run our business.

Though I had great difficulty communicating with the *"outside world"* during those days, I was experiencing an almost non-stop internal communication with the Spirit. Bible verses I had memorized and preached about for years now became truly alive. Passages that used to deeply worry me now became great promises. Words and phrases I thought I had understood began to take on very different meanings.

Peace, joy, grace, loving-kindness, holiness, sanctification, fruit of the Spirit, accepted into the Beloved, filled with the Spirit, rooted and grounded in love, abundant life, easy and light, confidence with God; I could go on and on, and I will in this book. These concepts, and many others, came alive to me in ways I never experienced through my theological study. What I thought I had already learned, I suddenly *"knew"* deep within my being. I was encountering God. And I was captured with an overwhelming confidence that He was going to enable me to find and live that *easy* and *light* life Jesus promised!

I am not trying to be sensational just to sell another book *(apparently you already have this one)* but there are no other words to describe it; I was encountering God. The Holy Spirit was *"revealing Jesus to me"*. Although there have been many levels of intensity and a wide variety of expression over the years that followed those days in January and February of 1997, that encounter has never really stopped. Perhaps it has just matured. I would like to think that is true.

I have no real explanation for exactly what happened to me and I certainly have no answer to the question, *"Why me?"* I wasn't fasting and praying harder than other people. In fact, I had given up. Nor do I hold up my personal experience as any kind of a model to follow. I have learned that we each have our own journey in God and He knows exactly how we should be led in our search to encounter Him. And as Paul warned us, *"comparing ourselves among ourselves"* (2 Cor. 10:12) is not smart.

But I do know some of the results that have come into my life. I know that the very foundation for my life and faith has been changed. *"Christ in me"* (Col. 1:27) has become a reality I experience daily and *"fellowshipping the Father"* (1 John 1:3) has become a very normal thing in my life. And I believe the purpose for this incredible journey has been, not the weird experiences I have had, but the life-altering truths I have learned. At least I think I have learned something important. When you finish reading this book I will let you be the judge for yourself.

As a direct result of this life-changing encounter, my wife and I gave up our home and everything we owned. We reduced our lives to two suitcases each, and have lived the last several years constantly *"on the road"*, from state to state and country to country, helping others in their own search to encounter God. I am inviting you to join me in that same search through the pages of this book.

But as we start this search together, we have to begin by admitting that something is missing, something is wrong.

Something Is Wrong

I was radically born again as a young, long-haired hippie in 1967. Now in January 1997, after nearly thirty years, I was hurting badly enough to run the risk of admitting something was seriously wrong. I had been a pastor, teacher, conference leader, missionary and church consultant for most of my life. But something was wrong. Some very basic element inside of me was *"out of whack"*.

I was not getting the results in my personal life that the Bible seemed to clearly say I should have been getting. And I hadn't been getting the right results for many years. My awareness of this internal failure had been growing for the past five years and had now resulted in mental and emotional meltdown.

Oh, I had experienced results, miraculous results: in finances, healing, divine interventions and supernatural answers to prayer. My ministry was doing well. People seemed to really like me and benefit from my work. I was helping lots of people succeed. But there was something very basic inside me that was just not right.

In my personal Bible study, these two words, *peace* and *joy,* kept catching my attention…and irritating me. I didn't have much of either one. I had a reasonable confidence about my salvation and eternal destiny, but peace and joy seemed to come and go depending on the current circumstances. Each time I read the Bible I found the New Testament believers talking about *unshakable peace* and *unwavering joy*, usually in the midst of terrible trials that God often didn't miraculously fix for them. And they seemed to live in this life of *peace and joy* even though they frequently were not experiencing what I would have defined as the *"victorious Christian life"*. I had to admit that my own experience just didn't line up with theirs.

Jesus talked about a life where His followers would regularly have encounters with the Father, *and actually know Him as their Father!* He promised a life that would revolve around the simple activity of watching the Father's lead and following it (John 16:13). *No pressure, just watch and follow.* He said we were so valuable to the Father that we wouldn't have to agonize over how our needs would be met (Matt. 6:31, 10:31). He talked about a river of living water that would flow out of the inner most part of His followers and that this living water would satisfy their deepest cravings (John 7:38). He said a principle job of the Holy Spirit would be to keep revealing both Jesus and the Father to believers in ways they could see, feel and understand (John 16:14). And He regularly held out the promise that this new kind of life would be abundant, all sufficient, completely fulfilling, satisfying the deepest hunger of those who would follow Him. I didn't have that kind of a Christian-life experience.

Jesus certainly talked about struggle and tribulation, family turning against family and being mistreated because we were misunderstood. Yet, He seemed to say that this *internal* life would be so *easy* and *light* that it would overshadow all *external* challenges. But when the circumstances of my life got really rough, I saw that I was missing something very basic in my understanding of what Jesus actually meant about this *"abundant life"*.

Things got bad enough that I was finally able to take my *"minister's mask"* off and admit that I had actually been having this struggle for years. And for years, I kept telling myself that it would all change as I *"grew up in Christ"*. I kept reassuring myself that I just needed to become more *"mature in God"*. I needed to learn more, I needed to memorize more and I would experience more faith. And somehow that would produce more peace and joy.

But it didn't. As the years went by I studied more, I learned more, and I memorized more; in more translations and in original languages. But consistent *peace* and *joy* did not increase along with my knowledge.

9

More Knowledge Only Made It Worse

In fact, the more I learned, the worse it became. The more I learned about the things Jesus said, the more troubled I became about the life I was experiencing. I am not talking about some gross sin or perversion. I am talking about a real lack of consistent *peace and joy.* I am talking about my inability to be *"anxious for nothing"* (Phil. 4:6) and to live with a confidence that His love for me was truly unconditional because I really was *"more valuable to Him than the sparrows"* (Matt. 10:31). Some essential ingredient was missing.

My own experience was not *"easy and light"*. Perhaps you can identify with my struggle. The longer I had been a Christian, the harder it became. The older I got, the more I learned. The more I learned, the more I had to do. The more I had to do, the more condemned I felt for not doing all I knew I was supposed to do. Instead of enjoying any progress I made, I felt guilty about all I knew I should be doing but I was not yet doing perfectly. *Easy and light?* It seemed to me that this life had gotten harder and heavier the further I went.

It has taken me years to be able to admit this without expecting to hear thunder roll in the distance as the anger of a Holy God gathered lightning over my head. But when you get desperate enough, honesty becomes your only hope.

This book is an attempt to share my journey as it unfolded, and I invite you to walk along with me on the road to honest discovery. If Jesus is indeed the Way, the Truth and the Life, then He surely invites honest seekers to ask honest questions; and He must be willing to meet them with honest answers. They rarely come when I want them to, the way I want them to; but I have found that the answers do come.

I have been around long enough to know the old song that says, *"Every day with Jesus is sweeter than the day before."* And I finally became honest enough to say it had not been that way for me very often. I knew it was not His fault, it was mine…somehow. I just didn't know how.

The more I learned about the life the early believers lived, the more I realized I didn't have what they had. The more I read what Paul wrote about the fruit of the Spirit, the more frustrated I became with my lack of that kind of amazing fruit. The more I read what Peter wrote about having *"joy unspeakable and full of glory"* (1 Peter 1:8), the more I became convinced something fundamental was missing inside of me.

Peace And Joy, Not Free Of Pain

I have studied enough about the first century believers to know they suffered horribly. I doubt it's possible for us, in western culture, to begin to understand the pain and anguish they endured. By *"easy and light,"* I know Jesus did not mean *"free of pain"*. He said that *"in this world you will suffer tribulations"* (John 16:33). He said, *"Watch what happens to the teacher and know that these things will happen to the student as well"* (John 15:18). Paul, Peter, James and John all wrote that suffering is part of living in this fallen world, and it will be *"until the restoration of all things"* (Acts 3:21). They even went so far as to boldly say that suffering was part of entering into the kingdom and that we must learn to rejoice in our trials, knowing the valuable results they will produce for us (Acts 14:22, James 1). Yet, in all Jesus suffered, He lived an *"easy and light"* life of obedience to the Father. No struggle, no fear and no condemnation.

After years of frustration, I was no longer after a life where God is my *heavenly butler* just waiting to fix everything so I am never bothered by the troubles of life. I had tried that long enough to know He wouldn't do it anyway, no matter how much faith I claimed to have. I had no illusions that one day I would obtain such great faith that all troubles and trials would cease to exist. Nor did I think that's what Jesus was offering.

But I know what I <u>am</u> after; a life full of *unshakable peace* and *abounding joy*. I am after true, divine *peace* and *joy* that is not dependent on my immediate circumstances but enables me to live the *easy* and *light* life, even when circumstances don't change. *No, especially when they don't change!* And I want to be consistently growing in Christ-likeness without feeling condemned and rejected every time I miss the mark.

But I have been at this Christian life for a long time. I have read many books, attended many conferences and heard many sermons. I have amassed so many notes on the *"Keys to This"* or the *"Secret to That"*. I have preached about those *"secrets"* and written about those *"keys"*. And my spiritual *"to do list"* of the things I must do in order to become a real *"man of God"* is so long, I will need the Book of Revelation's 1000 year millennial reign of Christ just to get it all done. Just looking at that *"to do list"* makes me feel pretty hopeless and makes me wonder *what's wrong with me*.

I know what I am after in God but I also know there is obviously something wrong with me. But what is it? My wife has been lovingly asking me this for years, and with very good reason.

"So, just what <u>is</u> wrong with me?"

Great. So now I am talking to myself.

Chapter Two

Now I'm Talking To Myself

It might help if you understood a little more about me and how I became obsessed with this search for the *"easy and light"* life Jesus promised.

A Reluctant Charismatic

I would reluctantly describe myself as a Charismatic Christian. I am a *"charismatic"* because I do believe that the presence, power, and miraculous gifts of the Holy Spirit are alive and working through people today. I say *"reluctantly"* because I have real problems with some of the teaching that goes on in certain charismatic circles. I try to not be too judgmental when I disagree with others because, as you will see in this book, I am learning that I frequently don't agree with myself!

Some charismatic teaching is just shallow and misleading. But some of it is dangerous and results in much unnecessary pain and confusion. I am sometimes embarrassed by the antics of my more *"charis-maniac"* friends. But, in the interest of full disclosure, I have sometimes been embarrassed by my own antics in my personal search for the invisible God.

But I have to admit it: I love the Holy Spirit. I love the *"goose bumps"*. I love passionate worship. I can be quiet and contemplative, but I thoroughly enjoy it when our love is loud and our worship is big. I think of myself as being *"seeker-sensitive"* but only if the seeker is truly after a life-changing encounter with the Living God. Encountering God does, by its very definition, involve an element of *"weirdness"*. *He is God, after all!* And I do love the *"weirdness"* of true God-encounters.

I have been at this long enough to know that really hungry people, truly starving people don't wait patiently in the buffet line. They will do anything to get to the food that will keep them alive. And their actions may offend others who are not as hungry. I have traveled around the world and I have seen what people will do to keep from starving to death. I have never done most those things. But I have never been that hungry.

I cannot escape the truth that David spoke of when he said, *"As the deer pants for the water brooks, so my soul pants for You, O God. My soul thirsts for God, for the living God"* (Ps 42:1-2 NAS). The deer he refers to is not seeking just a cool, refreshing drink. It is not seeking water to just quench its thirst. This deer is seeking water to keep from dying. There is a desperation here for the *"living God"* that I think my heart is familiar with, but my mind just does not fully understand.

I do know it can be a dangerous thing to pass judgment on someone else's desperation or try to interpret their attempts to reach God. The woman with the issue of blood, Blind Bartimaeus, the woman pouring oil on Jesus' feet, the screaming crowds as Jesus entered the city on a donkey, and the list goes on and on; they were all criticized by the disciples or the Pharisees for over-reacting, for being too loud or too emotional. But neither the disciples nor the Pharisees understood the *"heart-desperation"* these people were experiencing. They couldn't see inside so they passed judgment on the actions they could see on the outside.

I have been guilty of that kind of judgment. It's not a good thing to do. I remember an experience with the Lord where I distinctly sensed Him say to me, *"It is not a question of whether you are still a Pharisee, Mark. It's a question of how much of a Pharisee are you, still?"*

I know what it is like to encounter the Spirit, to be *"filled to overflowing"* and become lost in His presence. Since 1967, I have experienced (and survived) major and minor *"moves of the Spirit"* or *"times of renewal"*. From the Jesus Movement, to the Denominational Charismatic Renewal, to the Catholic Charismatic Renewal, to remaining pockets of the Latter Rain Movement, to the Word of Faith Movement, to the Discipleship Movement, to the Laughing Revival, the Toronto Blessing and the many variations of each; and many others too small to have an official name. Though I deeply appreciate every encounter I have had with the Holy Spirit, until I started this journey in 1997, they had all left me wondering why I was not able to *"abide in Him"* (John 15:4). The problem was not ultimately with any *"movement"*; the problem was in me and my concept of God.

I realize the *"tide ebbs and flows,"* *"seasons come and go,"* and you can't *"live on the mountain top"* all the time. I have preached all those sermons. But I have been desperately searching for a way to become a *"habitation for God"* (Eph. 2:22). I am on a journey to find the kind of life Jesus talked about where I *abide in Him* and He *abides in me* (John 15:4). I have gotten tired of having temporary visitations that left me essentially unchanged. I am not ungrateful, I am just tired of trying so hard and coming up empty; and I know it's my fault, not His.

However, I no longer wonder about most of those things because I have found some genuine answers! And though I am not experiencing the *"fullness"*, and I know we can't experience all of

15

God in this present life, I *am* living in a very real measure of *peace*, *joy* and *"presence"* I never thought was possible. I am living in an ongoing encounter with God that I...Oops! I'm getting ahead of myself. Sorry. Now back to our journey.

OK, So I Talk To Myself

I really started to get into trouble when I began admitting that I did, indeed, seriously lack abiding peace and joy. Not admitting it out loud, you understand. Not actually telling anyone. Not even admitting it in actual prayer. Just thinking about it. Just talking to myself about it. These are not the types of questions leaders want to ask out loud. It tends to make the followers nervous. So I just talked to myself.

Then I started asking myself if what I was experiencing was really what the Christian life was supposed to be. I got into deeper trouble when I began asking myself if the quality of life I have been experiencing actually lived up to the advertising I did about it in my public ministry. I was traveling around the world declaring the peace and joy God wants to give us through Jesus.

But in my *"heart of hearts"*, I had to admit I was very confused about some of the most basic concepts of what the Bible teaches are essential to living life in the New Covenant. I had my theology clear and concise. I just couldn't get it to produce the *unwavering peace* and *unshakable joy* those early believers wrote about.

I Don't Understand These Terms

I began to suspect that my problem had to do with my lack of understanding of what the Bible writers meant when they used certain words. Not the Hebrew or Greek meanings but what these concepts actually meant in their daily lives. Much to my embarrassment, I had to admit I didn't truly understand terms like *"New Covenant"*. What does that actually mean? What did Jesus mean when He used that term? Theologically, I can explain it. But I was not living in it. Not really. The evidence that I was not living in it was the obvious lack of *New Covenant fruit* in my life. What value is there in being able to explain something if I can't get it to work in my life?

Once I became honest enough to start asking myself these questions, then other words and phrases began to trouble me. What did Jesus mean when He said the greatest commandment was to *"love God"* and if you do this *"one thing"* then all the other commandments would naturally be fulfilled in your life? What could that mean? Paul said the same thing when he wrote *"Love fulfills the Law"* (Rom. 13:10). It just sounds way too simple.

And what was that *"one thing"* Paul said he put <u>all</u> his confidence in? (Phil. 1:6) What enabled him to describe the horrible sufferings he went through as being only *"momentary, light afflictions"*? (2 Cor. 4:17) What produced the *"joy unspeakable and full of glory"* in people whom Peter said were going through horrible *"fiery trials"*? (1 Peter 1:6-8) What did Jesus mean when He said *"apart from Me you can do nothing"*? (John 15:5) How would my life look if I really believed and experienced that?

How could Paul say that he sometimes failed to do the things he knew he should do, and he sometimes did things he knew he should not do...yet he had no condemnation in his life? (Rom. 7-8) Doesn't that kind of thinking lead to careless, loose living? Could Peter have been serious when he said we can be *"partakers of the divine nature"*? (2 Peter 1:4) And how would that look in my daily life?

Does this divine nature have something to do with the fruit of the Spirit? And if it's the Spirit's fruit then why am I working so hard to produce it and still falling so miserably short of the goal? And why is it that when I try my hardest to make myself more holy all I seem to get is...*tired*?

My Biggest Dilemma

Without question, my biggest struggle has been over Jesus' declaration to the hard-working, God-fearing Jews that He came to bring a lifestyle that would be *"easy and light"* (Matt. 11:30). And what about His claim that this *New Way* of living would produce *rest*? Jesus was not giving an altar invitation to rank heathens when He said this. He was speaking to God's worn out people inviting them into a *New Way* of living that would be *easy* and *light*.

John seemed to be talking about this *"easy and light"* way of living when he wrote about how natural it should be to confess our sin and to live a life full of confidence at the same time. Confession and confidence. Those are two words I rarely used together. When I had to confess my sin I usually lost my confidence with God, at least for a while. When I would really mess up and finally confess, I felt terrible for a few days. Then gradually my confidence would return. John seemed to do just the opposite. He spoke about being able to freely confess and not lose confidence with God.

I have struggled for years with John's statement that *"if our hearts do not condemn us then we have confidence with God"* (1 John 3:21). I could not understand how to live so my heart did not condemn me. It didn't seem possible. In my way of thinking, the only way for my heart to not condemn me was to live without sin. And it didn't look like that was going to happen any time soon!

18

John linked confession of sin and confidence together and seemed to feel good about it. I just could not understand what he meant.

The Old And The New

Paul constantly wrote about the difference between the Old Covenant and the New Covenant. He seems to be saying that understanding the difference between the *Old Way* and the *New Way* is the key to living this *"easy and light"* life. He certainly warned people about the danger of forsaking the *New* and returning to the *Old*. Since I assumed the *New Way* was *"receiving Jesus as my personal Savior"*, and I knew I understood that, I couldn't figure out what he meant and why it was so important to him.

The people Paul wrote to still believed in Jesus. They were still trusting Jesus for their salvation. But he said that by looking for rules and commandments they were *"falling from grace"* (Gal. 5:4) and they were in danger of *"making the grace of God of no effect"* (Gal. 2:21). He almost angrily told them this was because they were turning away from the *"New Way"* and returning to the *"Old Way"*. I no longer thought I understood what he was so upset about.

The further I go in this journey the more I see a clear connection between the *New Way* Jesus spoke about and the word, *grace*, which Paul used constantly. I am not sure what the connection is but I know it's there somewhere. Paul began and ended nearly every letter with this word *grace*. He claimed that everything he had accomplished was the result of the *grace* of God at work within him (1 Cor.15:10). Peter said we were to *"fix our hope completely"* on the *grace* of God and that we were to learn what *"true grace"* is and learn to *"stand firm in it"* (1 Peter 1:13, 5:12). Apparently, both Paul and Peter thought we might not understand what *"true grace"* meant.

I May Have Found My Problem

I am starting to get a bit nervous because after all these years of theological study I am no longer certain that I know what *"grace"* actually means. I thought it meant *"unmerited favor"* which to me had become *"God loves you no matter how much of a screw-up you are"*. But that doesn't seem to be what the New Testament leaders were talking about at all. As I read all their references to *"grace"*, I get the idea that this word was very important to them. It seems to be a powerful word, a life-changing word.

I have always thought *grace* and *mercy* were pretty much the same thing. But it doesn't look like the early believers thought that way at all. I am no longer sure that what I mean when I say *"grace"* is what they meant when they said *"grace"*.

I may have stumbled upon my real problem. If I don't understand what they meant by some of these important words they used, how can I ever understand what they meant by the *"New Way"*? And if I don't understand the *New Way* how can I ever hope to find the *"easy and light"* life Jesus promised?

I am beginning to suspect this search is going to require a whole new list of *biblical definitions*.

Chapter Three

Is It This Or Is It That?

There is a now infamous (or humorous, depending on your political persuasion) moment in US history when a sitting president was being impeached for lying to a grand jury about an alleged sexual encounter with a White House aide. When asked if he had actually made a particular statement, he responded with the defense, *"That depends on what your definition of the word 'is' is."*

I doubt that I was the only American to groan at this response. Although, I admit in my nearly six decades of living, I have used similar tactics to hopefully avoid the consequences of some of my own actions. The point, of course, was clear: it all depends on how you define something.

Definition means everything, or causes something to mean nothing. Definition tells me what to do, or not do. It tells me what I can safely touch, or what I better not touch. It tells me what to expect, or not expect. And in human relations, it tells me how I can communicate and relate to another person. The definition of something tells me what I can expect, what I can believe, what I can trust in...or what I should avoid or beware of.

Wrong definition may be merely humorous: the young boy who sneaks into his father's bathroom to attempt his first time shaving and begins by gyrating around the room because the label on the can of shave cream said *"shake well before using".*

Wrong definition may be sad, such as watching the President of the United States quibble about the word *"is"* rather than just saying *"I was wrong".*

Or it could be deadly: a parent misunderstands the instructions on the prescription bottle and innocently gives the child a deadly dose of a powerful medicine. It doesn't matter how sincere they are in their love for the child and their desire to do the child good. Definition causes us to act in a certain way, and those acts bring consequences. Wrong definition can result in sincere people having to pay a terrible price.

Peace and Joy Depend On The Right Definition

I strongly suspect, for the believer, there is no more important misunderstood word in the Bible than the word *"grace".* For the person who wants to grow in God, fulfill their divine destiny, and experience a life of unshakable peace and abounding joy, the true definition of grace is absolutely essential.

The difference in a life of guilt, regret, and frustration, or a life of peace, joy, and fulfillment may well come down to how I define *"grace".* A life of condemnation and shame about all the ways I am not yet like Christ, or a life of exciting expectation about the changes that are occurring within me on my journey in God is almost always the result of how I define *"grace".*

Whether I truly believe *"He who is in me is greater than he who is in the world,"* or I am just hoping against hope that God will somehow overlook the fears that riddle my daily life, does not really depend on how hard I can confess that Bible verse, but on how I define that little five letter word, *"grace".*

Of course, most of us who have spent any time in church think we know what grace is. We talk about it, *"I know I am not all I should be but thank God for His grace"*. We sing about it, *"Amazing grace, how sweet the sound."* We are grateful when we think someone has shown it to us, *"I really messed up and thoughtlessly hurt that person but they are so full of grace they forgave me, I am grateful they showed me grace."* And all these things are good, better than good, they are great. *They are just not actually "grace"*. If I think they are, I am guaranteed to miss the amazing benefits of *true grace* the way the early believers benefited from it.

Is It *This* or Is It *That?*

The devil's great weapon is deception. His power comes from leading people to believe that something is *this* when it is actually *that*; that something God says is wrong is actually right, that something God says will bring joy will just bring boredom, that something God says will bring peace will just bring pain, that something God says is good for us is somehow bad for us and that what Paul described as the *"simplicity of the Gospel of grace"* cannot be actually simple because there is so much I have to learn and do.

I have begun to suspect that the devil specializes in convincing me that the *simplicity* of the life Jesus described throughout His ministry is just too, well, *simple*. How can it be possible to actually live the *"easy* and *light* life" Jesus offered? In Matthew 11, Jesus says *"All of you who are worn down and worn out from trying to keep all the rules, come to me. If you will join with me you will find a life that is easy and light and you will enter into an experience called 'rest'"*. Sounds great, but it's just too simple.

23

What about all the other verses such as: *"You must be holy because I am holy"*, *"If you love me, you will prove it by keeping all my commandments"*, *"Without holiness no one will see God"*, *"If I regard any sin in my heart you will not hear my prayers"*, *"Work out your own salvation with fear and trembling"*. This certainly doesn't sound easy or light. And this is what the Bible says, right?

No, not really. These "verses", and many others similar to them, are not actually what the scripture teaches. In our repetition of these misquoted verses, we have either added or omitted important words. And far too often, these passages have been taken horribly out of context. I know. To my embarrassment, I have misquoted verses like these and preached on them many times over the years.

Getting Definitions Clear

One of the most basic rules in competitive debating is about what happens before the debate begins. The competitors get together and agree on the definition of terms that will be used in the course of the debate. Without this agreement on definition there can be no communication. Without clear definitions, there can be no substantive discussion, no understanding and no meaningful dialogue.

If I define something differently than God defines it, I cannot possibly understand what He is trying to communicate to me. If He cannot communicate clearly to me, I cannot possibly experience what He wants me to experience. If He says one thing, and I think He means something completely different, we cannot possibly have a good relationship; we cannot communicate.

I am not mechanical. Now there's an understatement. The only building project I ever undertook was a dog house for our family pet. When I finished, bruised and bandaged, the dog was too embarrassed to sleep in it. So if I help you work on your car, and you ask me for a particular tool, the odds are very good I will hand you the wrong one. Not because I don't want to help, but because I don't know what you mean. It's not that I don't want to work with Jesus; I just frequently don't understand what He means.

If I go ahead and hand you the wrong tool, it won't be out of rebellion or willful disobedience, it will be because I don't understand what you mean. It will be because my definition and understanding is different than yours. We can't communicate and work together because we have different definitions. If a carpenter tells me he needs a plane, there is a real good chance I will head for the airport. My life experience causes me to define certain things very differently than his.

I Don't Think The Way God Thinks

That's my problem with God; I don't think like He thinks. He told me that. *"For my thoughts are not your thoughts and my ways are not your ways"* (Isaiah 55:8). I don't understand things the way He understands them. He told me to *"Trust in the Lord's understanding of things and lean not to your own understanding"* (Pro. 3:5).

So I have to begin my journey by understanding...I don't understand Him. His words mean something different than my words.

But He also promised that if I will stick with Him and keep following after Him, His *"word will become a light to my path"* (Ps.119:105). Jesus promised that the Holy Spirit would be *"the Teacher"* and that one of His jobs is to *"guide us into all truth"* (John 16:13). So I reassure myself that it is possible to at least

25

begin to understand what He means when He says *"my way is easy and light and you can find this life of rest"* (Matt. 11:30).

Paul prayed for the people he ministered to that *"the eyes of their understanding would be opened that they might be able to comprehend"* (Eph.1:18, 3:18). On my journey to find that *"easy and light life"* where unshakable peace and unending joy are the normal experiences, regardless of circumstances, I see that I desperately need my eyes opened that I might be able to see how God defines the way, the truth and the life. And since the word *"grace"* was used so frequently by the apostles, I suspect I better get God's definition of *grace*.

One Thing, Just One Thing?

Paul understood something I am only just beginning to catch a glimpse of when he said *"I am confident of this <u>one thing</u>, that He who began the good work in you, He will complete it"* (Phil. 1:6). I shake my head and look at that again – *"I am confident of this one thing"*. *Just one thing*? And what is that one thing? *"He who began this, He will finish it"*.

Because I have spent most of my adult life reading the Bible, I immediately think of Heb. 12:2 – *"fixing our eyes on Jesus who is the author and finisher of our faith"*. The *"author"* of something is the *"starter, creator or originator"*. The Greek word used for *"finisher"* means *"completer or consummator"*. If He is the *"starter"* and the *"completer"* of my faith, then somehow this *easy* and *light* life must be about what He is doing within me instead of something I do. This seems to be very similar to the *"one thing"* in which Paul was so confident, that *He who began it, He will complete it*.

I am beginning to suspect this has something to do with the true definition of grace. I just don't know what it is, yet.

Could it be that by looking so much at my lack, my confusion and my inability, I have misunderstood where I should fix my eyes? Could I have been trusting in the wrong thing all these years? Could it be that since Jesus is the one who began this life in me, then the goal is to learn how to let Him complete it in me? And could this have something to do with *"grace"*?

Obviously, Paul's *"one thing"* has not been my *"one thing"*. But if it became my *"one thing"*, then I can see how that could result in an *"easy* and *light"* life. If I begin to define the Christian life as somehow learning to let Him live through me then I can see how this could result in the life of rest Jesus offered.

Could This Really Be True?

Could this be true, that the Christian life is all about what He is doing *in* us, *for* us and *through* us? Could this be a clue as to why Paul began and ended nearly every one of his letters with the word *"grace"*? Could this be why *grace* appears to be the central theme for everything Paul, Peter and the other early church leaders taught about the Christian life?

If this is true, then I am confronted with another obvious truth – I have been defining grace all wrong. Apparently, I do not know what *grace* actually means. Not the way God means it. And I suspect that is a good place to start.

Chapter Four

No, It's Not That...
Or That...Or That

I clearly have thought I knew what the word *grace* meant. But I am beginning to suspect I have been wrong because my definition has not produced what Jesus promised as an *"easy and light"* life. So let's begin with what I have been erroneously thinking and see how it measures up to the Biblical definition.

Grace Is Not Mercy

I am starting to see my most common mistake has been using the word *grace* when I actually mean *mercy*.

Mercy is absolutely essential. Mercy is the undeserved and unconditional love of God for us. It is the beginning of all relationship with God. And it is God's mercy towards us that always sustains our relationship with Him. You never *"outgrow"* mercy. *"God loved the world so much that He gave His Son."* Mercy is the expression of this inexplicable love God has for all people. But this is not *grace*.

There is no humanly understandable reason why a God who is so perfectly complete in every way, who needs absolutely nothing, would choose to create within Himself a desire to love us. And by *"us"* I mean walking, talking piles of dirt. That is the biblical definition of how Adam was made, gathering up the dust of the earth and then breathing into it. And it is that dust to which our bodies will return. And yet, He chooses to love these feeble creations.

And these creations almost immediately chose to rebel, disobey and to perpetuate disobedience and ingratitude throughout their generations. And yet, He loves the world, not the globe, but the people of the world, so much that He sacrificed the most precious part of Himself that some of those people, just some of them, might choose to love Him back.

**Mercy, the unconditional love of God,
is absolutely essential.**

But this is not grace.

More often than not when we use the word *grace* we actually mean *mercy*. *"I know I really messed up but thank God for His grace."* Of course what we mean is, *"Thank God for His mercy, thank God for His undeserved forgiveness"*.

"I know I didn't deserve to be forgiven but thank God for his grace." But we mean mercy. This is wonderful, amazing and essential, *but this is not grace*.

Paul clearly taught that we are saved *because* of God's mercy but we are saved *by* His grace. Eph 2:4-5 – *"But God, being rich in mercy, because of His great love with which He loved us, even when we were dead in our transgressions, made us alive together with Christ (by grace you have been saved)..."*.

Why did God do this?

Because He is rich in mercy towards us.

How did it happen?

By the power of His grace.

What made me alive in Christ when I was dead in my transgressions?

The power of God's grace.

On my journey to learn what Paul means when he talks about grace, I am starting to see –

1)	There is a big difference between *mercy* and *grace*.
2)	There is an important connection between *grace* and *power*.

Grace Is Not Forgiveness

This is closely connected to our thinking that grace and mercy must be the same thing. We are sinners separated from God. Christ dies for us, pays the entire penalty, and purchases our forgiveness and I say, *"Thank God for His grace"*. But I mean *"Thank God for His mercy."*

Mercy brings forgiveness. God's forgiveness of my sin says a lot about God's heart and nature, but it says nothing about mine. Being forgiven is no indication that something within me has changed.

Remember the parable Jesus taught about the man who owed a huge amount of money to a creditor and could not repay. The creditor had mercy on him and forgave him. But the forgiven man

31

turned around, found someone who owed him a small amount of money, and treated them terribly. Mercy alone didn't change him.

My debt has been forgiven but forgiveness alone does not change my nature. There is no indication that I am any different because of God's rich mercy shown by forgiving me. Paul spoke of more than just forgiveness. He spoke of having been dead but now being *"made alive in Christ"*. As I read what he said about being *"made alive"* I am beginning to suspect he was talking about power. It would require power to take what was dead and make it alive! Being forgiven is wonderful, amazing and essential. *But this is not grace.*

Grace Is Not "God Giving Us Time To Learn To Obey"

In my journey to understand what Paul meant when he spoke of *grace*, I have read many authors and listened to many teachers, and I am indebted to them all. Some for adding to a growing revelation in my heart and some for just articulating the same confusion I have struggled with. Both have been very valuable to me in my search for the *easy* and *light* life.

One phrase I heard a preacher use that really summed up much of what I had erroneously believed was, *"Grace is God giving us time to learn how to obey Him"*. Of course, this is just another way of saying *"Grace is mercy"*. This is the idea that grace is *"God overlooking our sin until we finally grow up and don't sin anymore"*.

This concept fit very well with my concept of the normal Christian life. I saw God as being rich in mercy and forgiving my transgressions at my conversion, and then handing me a Bible and telling me, *"Now hurry up and grow up so you can learn to do all this and finally make Me happy"*. My confidence was in asking

God to give me one more chance, and this time I will try harder and get it right.

Remember Paul saying he was confident in just *one thing*? His "one thing" was *"He who began this work in you, He will complete it"*. That was not my one thing. My one thing was, *"I promise I will try harder"*.

Welcome To The *"Promise Makers"* Club

For many years I have felt like a charter member of the *"Promise Makers"* Club. Not the *"Promise Keepers,"* that's a great organization. I am talking about the *"Promise Makers,"* an underground group with lots and lots of secret members.

You can find us in every church, at every prayer meeting, at every conference. We are deeply committed and very sincere. We are not causal Christians, we are *"soldiers in the army of the Lord"* and we are serious about this battle. We don't have a secret handshake or special badge, but we do have a special *"look"*. Because we *"Promises Makers"* are trying so hard to keep our promises to God we frequently look like we are, well, forgive my crudeness, but we frequently look like we are constipated.

We are trying so hard to *be* and *do* all we are supposed to *be* and *do*, we often look as if we are in pain. And, of course, we are in pain, the pain of constantly seeing our failures in spite of any progress we have made. We are in pain because we are really serious about obeying God and we feel really guilty about not obeying God...perfectly...now!

In our shame and pain we pray things such as, *"God, if you will forgive me one more time I promise this is the last time I will behave like that. I know the last time I did this I said that would be the last time. But I realize now that was actually the 'next to the last time'. I see now that this is actually the last time, I promise!"*

33

Of course, obeying God is biblical, it is right, and it certainly seems to be the goal. Over the many years I have been a pastor and teacher, I feel I have done a reasonably good job of telling Christians *what* they are supposed to *"be and do"*. But I am beginning to think I have done a terrible job of telling people *how* to *"be and do"*. I am starting to see that the members of the *"Promise Makers"* club know all about the *"what"* but it's the *"how"* that causes us all the pain.

As I progress on my journey towards God's definition of grace, I am beginning to suspect that true grace is all about *how* we can become more like Him, *how* we can learn to love like Him, and *how* we can be enabled to behave like Him. Could it be that grace is about how God empowers and enables humans with an ability greater than their own feeble promises? I thank God from the depths of my being that He gives me time to learn how to obey Him, but I am learning that is not grace. *It is mercy, it is amazing love, but it is not grace.*

Grace Is Not An Excuse For Bad Behavior

Perhaps one of the most damaging beliefs some people hold is that grace is the thing that enables God to overlook our bad behavior and excuse it: the belief that because of grace, somehow our bad behavior doesn't matter. We say things like, *"I know I am not all I should be but thank God for His grace."* I know most of us would never say out loud that our behavior doesn't matter, that our lack of obedience has no bearing on our walk with God or our relationship to other people. But somehow, when faced with our repeated failures at godliness, it's hard to not secretly hope God will accept His own love as an excuse and give us a free pass.

I confess that for many years I repeated the same advice I had been given by pastors older, and presumably, wiser than I was.

"Don't talk too much about grace or you'll give people the idea that they can live loose and carnal and it won't make any difference."

That was about the time I first heard the term *"greasy grace"*. It was always said with a little pastoral smirk and a wink of the eye as if to say we professional ministers were well aware that most people were looking for an excuse for their bad behavior. But at some point on this journey, I began to say, *"Wait a minute, a lot of God's people are doing a pretty good job of living loose and carnal without a clue as to what true grace means. Maybe if we truly understood grace it would help us all to actually live differently!"*

Of course, His mercy is everlasting and His love knows no end. Jesus died for all our sins and paid the penalty, once and for all. But being loved doesn't, in and of itself, empower me with divine ability. And being forgiven can free me from the past, but it does not change my nature, character or personality, which is my only hope of changing my future.

But this journey into grace offers far more than a *"fire escape"* for eternity. It offers an amazing possibility and promise about experiencing transformation in our lives here and now. *"For the grace of God has appeared, bringing salvation to all men, instructing* (enabling, empowering) *us to deny ungodliness and worldly desires and to live sensibly, righteously and godly in this present age..."* Titus 2:11-12. Paul seems to make it very clear that there is a way to actually live *sensibly and righteously*, now, *in this present age*, and that somehow that ability does not come from our power or our repeated and sincere promises. But, because of grace and whatever that really means, Paul says there is a power we can tap into that will enable us to say *"no"* to ungodliness.

That's what we members of the *"Promise Makers"* Club crave. We want to grow in Christ-likeness and live more godly lives…now. We desperately want to live a life that is pleasing to Him. Rather than grace being an excuse for bad behavior, I am beginning to suspect that true grace must somehow bring a power that can enable me to *"deny ungodliness"*. Paul says true Grace has the power to enable me to say *"no"* to what I couldn't say *"no"* to before, and *"yes"* to what I have wanted to say *"yes"* to all along.

So here we are again. Grace must have something very important to do with power. And not just some sort of nebulous power floating around in the air but *God's power inside of people*, people like you and me!

But wait a minute; doesn't grace mean *"unmerited favor"*?

Chapter Five

It's About Power...
I Think

As I travel and teach, I frequently ask my audience what they think the word grace really means. Without hesitation, those who have been in church very long will answer, as I always did, *"unmerited favor"*. As with many things in life, this is both true and untrue.

Grace Used To Mean Unmerited Favor

The Old Testament word for "grace" is used 240 times and is translated primarily as *"grace, favor, mercy, loving-kindness and steadfast love"*. This Hebrew word does indeed mean unmerited favor or undeserved love. It refers to how God felt about His people, that His love for them was unearned, it was undeserved, and came out of His nature, not in response to their nature. God's grace in the Old Testament (*unmerited favor*) was the loving-kindness He freely poured out on them because of who He was and how He felt about them. It was constant and unwavering because His nature is constant and unchanging.

But His *unmerited favor* could not truly change their nature. It could not empower them to live differently. The law could tell them *what* they were supposed to do to be like their God, but not *how* to become like Him. He continued to love them, and they continued to make sacrifices to cover their inability to live life as they should. And they had to live by faith that one day the Messiah would come and turn the promises into reality. Hebrews 11 tells us *"these all died in faith"*.

However, the New Testament word for *grace* means something very different. The words for mercy, favor and loving-kindness are certainly in the New Testament in abundance. But *grace* in the New Testament carries an entirely different meaning and this difference is the key to living full and free in the New Covenant.

So What Is The True Grace Of God?

John began his gospel with the announcement that *"The Law was given through Moses but grace and truth were realized through Jesus Christ"* (John 1:17-18). Peter gave an amazing description of what Christ wants to do in us and summed it up by saying *"...this is the true grace of God. Stand firm in it!"* (1 Peter 5:12). So what is the *"true grace of God"* we are supposed to *"stand firm"* in?

God's mercy and His unconditional love are major themes in the New Testament. In fact, the loving-kindness of the Old Testament was fully realized through what Christ did for us on the cross. The issue of God's unconditional love and unmerited favor on any one who will believe in Him is settled, once and for all, through the death and resurrection of Jesus Christ. But the Greek word, *charis*, used throughout the New Testament for "grace", is completely different. It always refers to God's power, and not just God's power, but *God's power in a person*. It is not a passive word, but an active word, a powerful word. *"Charis"* always carries the meaning of power coming *into* a person and flowing *through* them. It always refers to a power that will come from the outside into a person and enable them to live differently. To people like us, the members of the *"Promise Makers"* Club, this is more than just good news, this is a fantastic possibility!

True Grace Is About Power

We already know this word, *charis*. It forms the root word for an English word, *charismatic*. Charismatic means *"the continuation of the power and gifts of the Spirit"*. We get this meaning from another way the word *charis* is used in the New Testament. In 1 Cor. 12 Paul talks about the work of the Holy Spirit through miraculous *"gifts"* God invests in people.

Regardless of what we might believe about miracles today, in Paul's day, miracles happened. Not only did they happen, but they happened as the Holy Spirit caused the power of God to work *in* and *through* people. The word translated *"gift"* is the same word translated *"grace"*. This is an important clue in our journey to discover God's definition of *grace*.

Remember, *"charis"* is all about the power of God coming into and working through people. A New Testament gift of the Spirit was not a person's power but the power of God *in* a person. That means *grace*, the exact same word translated *"gift"*, is not about a person's power but God's power *in* a person.

I am a teacher so please indulge my repetition.

Grace = God's power working in and through a person.

Not my power or my promises, or my good intentions but God's power. And not just God's power in the universe, but God's power *in* me, working *through* me.

39

God's Power In and Through Me

Strong's Greek Dictionary defines *grace* as *"the divine influence in the heart and its reflection in the life."* It appears that the real definition of grace is about the power of God working in my heart and the result causes His nature to reflect out of me.

Imagine sunlight shining into a prism. The light comes in as one color, yellow light. But as it passes through, it breaks into every color of the spectrum and shines out onto other things in all its multi-colored brilliance. One influence shining in; resulting in many different influences shining out.

Could this be what Paul meant in Gal. 5:22, *"Now the fruit of the Spirit is love, joy, peace, patience, kindness, goodness, godliness, faithfulness and self-control"*? Could this be a word-picture from the Holy Spirit describing *grace*, the power of God, coming into my life, miraculously changing my heart and shining through me in the multi-colored light of the fruit of the Spirit? I think there is a clue here.

Remember, the Old Testament word for grace does mean, *"unmerited favor"*. But the New Testament word for grace means *"the power of God coming into a person and working through them, reflecting outward."* Grace is all about God's power working *in* me and then working *through* me.

Could this be why Paul would boldly say, *"I am confident of this one thing, that He who began this good work in you, He will complete it"*? It seems Paul, Peter, and John all knew something about the power of *grace* that I am just beginning to understand. Grace is not passive, *"Jesus loves me,"* but it is active, *"The Spirit's power is within me."*

The Master Deceiver's Master Plan

Peter makes some amazing statements about what Christ will do *in* us and then says this is the *"true grace"*. Apparently in his day there were already misconceptions about the real definition of grace. Of course, that makes sense. If grace is the power of God working in and through people, and if by trusting in this truth I can see it work in me, then the last thing the devil would want me to know is the definition of *true grace.*

Jude fully understood how destructive it was to twist or pervert the true meaning of grace. He warned the believers of his day that there were those who would come in among them who would seek to *"turn the grace of our God into licentiousness."* (Jude 4) He warned them that there would be people who would twist the meaning, destroy the value and even use their own definition as an excuse for the very thing grace is meant to empower us to say *"no"* to: ungodliness (Titus 2:11).

At the very least, a wrong definition of grace will leave us frustrated and confused, wondering why the Christian life doesn't seem to work right. At worst, it will leave us with a seared conscience and hard heart using the word *"grace"* as an excuse to justify willful and destructive sin.

Of course, the devil wants me confused about the true meaning of grace. It is the heart of the New Covenant. It is what makes the New Covenant *"new"*. It is the power of God that enables people to manifest the life of Christ through their life now. It is the ability from God to *"say no to ungodliness"*.

And it is the key to finding that *"easy and light"* life Jesus talked about as if it was just supposed to be the normal thing. If the enemy of our souls can reduce this powerful word to simply mean *"God loves us anyway"*, then we are stripping the New Covenant of the power Paul declared was our true hope in this life.

41

But I can't buy this grace, I can't qualify myself for it, and I can't earn it. To be frank, I don't like that. I want someone to tell me the keys, and I will work hard to do them. I want this thing to fit neatly into three, five or seven steps, and I would prefer they each start with the same letter of the alphabet. I am a teacher, after all. This way I can work on step one till I get it, then move on to step two in the hope I will finally be able to say, "*I did it!*"

But it just doesn't work that way. Because God really loves me, He keeps frustrating my human effort to *earn* His power in my life. He just won't allow me to *earn* this grace by my best effort.

So in my frustration, I cry out, *"Why not?",* and I think that's what He's wanting me to ask.

Chapter Six

It Can't Be Me
So It Must Be Him

Unearned Power

In my journey into true grace, I am learning that one thing about my mistaken definition of grace is absolutely true:

Grace, *the power of Christ in me*, must be <u>*unearned*</u>.

Both Old and New Testaments make it clear that any goodness, godliness, righteousness, holiness or sanctification must ultimately be the result of His work in me. None of these things can be earned, purchased, or produced by human effort.

The foundation for most of what we believe about salvation by grace comes from Eph. 2, *"For by grace you have been saved..."* But as with everything, we must see all He has to say about this truth to understand His definition. Without understanding His definition of truth, we cannot put our faith in Him and His work in us. This is the only way to have the confidence those early believers had.

Look closer at what Paul says to the Ephesians: *"For by grace you have been saved through faith; and that not of yourselves, it is the gift of God; not as a result of works, so that no one may boast"* (Eph.2:8-9). Paul makes it clear that this deal is all about His work and not ours, His power and not ours. Why? *So that no one may boast.* We are the recipients, the ones who benefit from His work, the containers for the fruit of His Spirit; but we cannot boast about producing it. He gets all the credit.

But I Want Some Credit

There is something about the fallen nature of man that drives us to crave the credit. This was the frustration of the Pharisees. They desperately wanted the credit for becoming godly. It drove them to wear special *"holy"* clothing so people would notice, pray loud prayers in public so people would notice, tie little boxes on their foreheads with small portions of Old Testament scripture inside so people would notice, blow a trumpet as they put their tithe in the offering box so people would notice, look hungry as they fasted so people would notice and go around in little groups of *"holy"* people, avoiding contact with the *"unholy"* common people, so people would notice. They craved the credit for what they hoped others would consider holy.

Could this be what drives me to *"humbly"* share with people how much I read the Bible, how much I give to missions, how hard I try to abide by the principles of godly living, how diligently I put into practice the Christian disciplines that will certainly result in all the blessings I want in this life? Of course, all these things are good and godly but I suspect my motive has a lot to do with who I am secretly hoping gets the credit.

44

No Room For Boasting

Paul repeatedly gave the example of Abraham being *"made righteous"* because he believed what God said about him. The Bible does not hide the fact that, throughout his walk with God, Abraham did several things right, and several things terribly wrong.

At least one thing Abraham did wrong is still affecting the world today. The descendants of Ishmael and Isaac are still fighting and regularly put the peace of the whole world in jeopardy. And yet, Paul says Abraham was made righteous, made right with God, because he believed what God said about him. To the Romans, Paul said God did this so there would be *no room for boasting.*

In Rom 3:27-28 Paul says *"Where then is boasting? It is excluded. By what kind of law? Of works? No, but by a law of faith."* To drive home the point even further, Paul continues in Rom 4:2-3 *"For if Abraham was justified by works, he has something to boast about, but not before God. For what does the Scripture say? 'Abraham believed God and it was credited to him for righteousness'."* (NAS)

Then Paul says we are Abraham's children if we believe what Abraham believed. But what did Abraham believe? He came to believe that God could and would do for him what he could not do for himself.

Abraham believed God would do for him what he could not do for himself; both in the spiritual realm, make him righteous, and in the natural realm, give him the promised son. But God did these things in a way that would prevent any boasting except boasting in the goodness and faithfulness of God. God did the work of making Abraham righteous. God also did the work of bringing forth a promised son to this old couple.

Could this be another important key to the true meaning of New Covenant grace: trusting God to do what I cannot do for myself both in the spiritual, eternal realm and in my natural, everyday life?

I crave an eternity with God, delighting in His unveiled presence and fulfilling my destiny in His eternal kingdom. But like you, I also crave to grow in His image and see His nature revealed more and more *through* me in this life. And there are many things I can do, many things I must do. But in this process of becoming more like Christ, there are things I just cannot do for myself.

Could This Issue Of Who Gets The Credit Unlock God's Grace?

Paul kept reminding his spiritual sons of how important this issue of credit really was. To his young leader, Titus, he said *"But when the kindness of God our Savior and His love for mankind appeared, He saved us, not on the basis of deeds which we have done in righteousness, but according to His mercy, by the washing of regeneration and renewing by the Holy Spirit, whom He poured out upon us richly through Jesus Christ our Savior..."* (Titus 3:4-6)

Can you hear Paul say there is no place for our boasting here? This is not about any good things we have done *in righteousness*. These deeds are the things we can do and should do as a *result* of the regeneration and renewing work the Spirit does in us. But these things don't produce regeneration and renewal. Grace is all about the power of His Spirit *regenerating* and *renewing* us regularly. And He wants to keep pouring out this great power upon us *richly*!

To his spiritual son, Timothy, Paul says, *"(He) has saved us and called us with a holy calling, not according to our works, but according to His own purpose and grace which was granted us in Christ Jesus from all eternity..."* (2 Tim 1:9).

Paul had been a *"Pharisee of the Pharisees"*. He became an expert on the Old Testament. When writing to Timothy, he refers to God's plan *"from all eternity"*. God has always worked so He would get all the credit.

To the Israelites in the wilderness He said that He was driving out the nations before them to fulfill the promise He made to Abraham, not because of their righteousness, because *"you are a stubborn people"* (Deut.9:4-6). To Gideon He said, *"You have too many men. If I let you win, you will think you did this by your power"* (Judges 7:2). To prove His point He commanded Gideon to reduce his army from many thousands to just 300. Forever after that battle, Jewish children were taught that God did it this way so they would only boast of His power and His great love for them. They were the beneficiaries of God's power at work for them. Their only boast was in Him.

There is no room for boasting when God works this way, except for boasting in the goodness and faithfulness of our great God. Through the revelation of *grace*, Paul understood God has always worked this way.

The beauty of this is that our confidence can now rest in Him, in His power and in His great love for us. Not in our ability to make better promises to Him, but in His ability to keep the promise He has made to His Son, and to us because we are in His Son.

Saved By Grace But Living By Works

I tell myself I am just trying to obey, but I keep falling into a trap. When things work out well, I feel compelled to share with others how I did the right things and the right things happened; and if they will just do the right things the right way then they, too, will

47

get the right things. Doesn't this definition of how good things happened for me have something to do with credit? Isn't there room here for boasting because of human effort?

But when things don't work out well, when crisis comes, when adverse circumstances befall me, my first questions are, *"What have I done wrong? Where did I miss the will of God? Why didn't I pray harder, read more, try harder? That's what I will do, I will read even more, I will pray even more, I will try even harder to be like God, try harder to make myself like Christ."*

In Joyce Meyer's book, *If Not For The Grace Of God*, she refers to the trap of knowing we are *"saved by grace but living by works"*. This happens when we know our salvation was a gift through the power of the cross but we continue to believe that God's daily love, acceptance and help depends on our good works being perfectly good. This truly describes my frustration and the trap I keep falling into as *Old Way* thinking trips me up.

Am I the only one who finds myself *"re-dedicating my re-dedication"*? Am I the only one who keeps trying to make bigger and better promises to God? Welcome to the *"Promise Makers"* Club; we have saved a seat for you.

But I Don't Want My Salvation To Depend On My Works!

Of course, I don't feel this way about salvation. I know there is nothing I can do that would pay for my sin, my separation from God. I know I am saved by unearned grace. I know it wasn't just His undeserved love that has canceled my sin and made me alive in Christ. It was His *power* at work within me. I know He deserves all the credit for this amazing salvation.

But, somehow, I have separated the eternal work He did in saving me, from the *transforming* work I long to see done in me now. I have fallen into the trap of believing salvation is by His grace, but successful Christian living must be the result of my works, my efforts, and my promises. So here I am again, *saved by grace but trying to live by works.*

The more I read what the Bible really says, the more I see the kind of life I am living cannot be the *New Covenant* way. This cannot be the *"easy and light"* life Jesus said was available to me. My human effort runs out way too soon and I am left frustrated and condemned.

If much of what I am doing is not producing New Covenant results, perhaps I don't understand the New Covenant at all.

So here I go again, I need a *new definition* of the New Covenant.

Chapter Seven

What is the New Covenant, Really?

All four Gospel writers recorded what took place around the table that we call the Last Supper. Of course, those guys didn't realize it was *the* last supper. If they did, I suspect they would have taken better notes.

Luke is the one who records Jesus as saying *"This cup which is poured out for you is the new covenant in My blood"* (Luke 22:20). As New Testament believers, the meaning of these words, *"the New Covenant"*, seems pretty obvious to us. However, as we are beginning to see on this journey into true grace, we may be mistaken. But to those guys, on the other side of the cross, these words, *"the New Covenant"*, had to mean something very different.

Huh?

As Jewish men, the 12 had been taught the meaning of the Covenant from their earliest memories. It wasn't the *"Old Covenant"* to them, it was the only Covenant. The laws of this Covenant governed their every moment, from the way they prayed, the way they ate, the way they washed their hands, the way they treated each other, to the way they thought about God.

But Jesus had been challenging all of those deeply ingrained beliefs. Nearly everything He taught seemed new or different. It had to be very confusing to them. In fact, when you read the four Gospels, you realize their most common response to most of Jesus' teachings was, *"Huh?"* That makes me feel a lot better.

The great explanations of many of the parables Jesus gave were a result of the disciples saying, *"We don't understand. Could you go over that one more time?"* That gives me great hope. If the guys who were right there with Him had a hard time understanding, I feel a bit better in my struggle to understand. After all, He did come to bring something new, something "better", based on better promises (Heb. 7). By its very definition, the *"new"* will be very different from the *"old"*.

But I suspect I don't understand this *New Covenant* much more than they did that night. I am beginning to see that I am living in the New Covenant concerning where I find my forgiveness, in Jesus, but I tend to live in the Old Covenant when it comes to how I walk each day, trying to please God by the strength of well-intended human effort. I find I am *"saved by grace but living by works"*. And I suspect it's because, like them, I don't really understand what He meant by the things He said as they sat around that table. I still view His words through the Old Covenant, the *Old Way* of thinking.

What Happened Around That Table?

John gives the most detailed description of what Jesus said that night. There are 21 chapters in the Gospel of John. Chapters 1-12, about half the letter, tell of the life and ministry of Jesus. Chapters 13,14,15,16 and 17 all take place around the table and on the short walk to the garden. John goes into great detail telling us what Jesus said in those few hours because, in these words, we find the heart of the New Covenant.

The tendency is to think the New Covenant is all about forgiveness. *"This is the new covenant in my blood, take this bread and this wine into yourself,"* He said. His body and blood were the sacrifice so the New Covenant must primarily be about forgiveness, right? It seems logical. Under the Old Covenant we think about people going to the high priest for sacrifice and forgiveness. Under the New Covenant we go to our high priest, Jesus. So the New Covenant must be about forgiveness. *But what if it is so much more?*

The Sacrifice That Completed the Old Covenant

Forgiveness has always been absolutely essential. But, in fact, the sacrifice of Jesus as the Lamb of God was the fulfillment and completion of the Old Covenant promise. Every sacrifice of the Old Covenant was fulfilled in the offering of Jesus for the sins of the whole world. Every Old Testament believer looked forward to the completion, the fulfillment of what they believed, every time they made a sacrifice.

When John the Baptist spoke of the Lamb of God, he was declaring God would complete the full forgiveness He promised in the Old Covenant through this perfect Lamb, once and for all. This fulfillment would no longer be the *covering* of sin but the *removing* of sin. Paul says this was accomplished by Jesus being *"made to be sin"* for us. This fulfilled the promise of the Old Covenant. It closed the chapter of *"looking forward to a better promise"*.

Reading all Jesus said around that table about the nature of the New Covenant in His blood, we begin to suspect He was speaking of much more than just a new way of forgiveness. Forgiveness is essential. But we have already begun to see that forgiveness alone doesn't change the nature of a man.

Jesus was speaking about something far better than just forgiveness. He was inaugurating a New Covenant that would not *"cover sin"* as the Old Covenant did, but this *New Way* would have the power to actually *make people new*. This is the amazing truth about grace. It has the power to transform, to make new!

What Do You Mean, You Are Going Away?!

The most disturbing thing Jesus said around that table was *"I am going away"*. It seems clear they heard very little after that early statement. John describes the confusion the disciples experienced. John 13:33-36, 14:5, 16:16-18 gives us much of the conversation.

> *"I have been telling you all along but now I tell you plainly, I am going away."* *"What do you mean, you are going away? We are going with you."* *"No. I must leave but you can't go with me now."* *"You can't leave us now, we are just about ready to take over".* *"I have to go away but you will be with me one day."* *"Well, we want to go with you now."* *"You can't, but you do know the way I am going."* *"We have no idea where you are going so how can we know the way?"* *"I am the way."* ***"Huh?"*** *"A little while and you won't see me, then a little while and you will see me."* ***"Huh?"***

Then, to really mess with their heads, He says, *"By the way, it is good for you that I go away."* *"HUH?!"*

This had to be more than confusing; it had to be down right scary! They had given up everything for this man whom they had come to see as the Messiah. Or as Peter put it in one of his few inspired moments, *"You are the Christ, the Son of God"*. This was what they had been looking for all their lives, all their parent's lives, all their grandparents' lives, all their great grandparents' lives...you get the picture. This was *"The Man"*. They had been talking *"kingdom talk"* for over three years and now the *"king"* says, *"I am leaving you and it's good for you that I leave"*.

Clearly, they heard nothing else, because, in this confusing conversation, is the very core of the New Covenant, the mystery of the ages, God's *Brilliant Plan*, the most amazing strategy ever conceived, the one thing those men wanted more than anything else.

This conversation contained the plan of God the prophets had spoken about. But they could not have had a clue how God would do it. Peter said the angels caught a glimpse of this plan in the ages before creation, and they could not understand how it could ever happen. The dark rulers of this world could not conceive of this *Brilliant Plan*, for if they had, they would have never crucified the Lord of Glory. All of history, in the endless ages past, looked forward to the unveiling of this *Brilliant Plan*.

Could This Brilliant Plan Be So Simple?

This *Brilliant Plan* is the New Covenant. And Jesus explained it all sitting around that table. He laid it out in just a few easy words. It seemed so simple, perhaps too simple for us humans to grasp without divine revelation.

Listen to Jesus as He says, *"It is good for you that I go away, because if I don't go, the Holy Spirit cannot come. And you know Him for He has been with you but He shall be in you. I am leaving but I will not leave you as orphans, I will return by my Spirit and live in you"* (John 14:16-18). Notice what may well be the most important little word in the Bible – *"in"*. *"He has been with you but He shall be in you. If I go away I will return by my Spirit and live in you"*. I am starting to see something here. Could the difference between the Old and the New be found in these two little words – "*on*" and "*in*"?

Listen to Jeremiah's prophesy about something he could not have possibly understood from his Old Covenant perspective – "*'Behold, days are coming,' declares the LORD, 'when I will make a new covenant with the house of Israel and with the house of Judah, not like the covenant which I made with their fathers... But this is the covenant which I will make with the house of Israel after those days,' declares the LORD, 'I will put My law within them and on their heart I will write it...'*" (Jer. 31:31-33).

What was the Old Covenant He made with their fathers? God put His expectations *on* stone. What is the New Covenant? God will put *Himself in* people.

But how can He do that?

Jesus died, was buried, rose again, ascended to the Father and sent the Holy Spirit to live *in* us! Not just be with us, but live *in* us! This is what the angels could not figure out. How could the God of indescribable power and unapproachable majesty live in a frail creation, in walking, talking, piles of dirt?

Here is God's *Brilliant Plan*, His divine strategy. Paul described it over and over again as the mystery of the ages – <u>*Christ in you, the hope of Glory*</u>!

What If He Didn't Go Away?

Just imagine what would have happened if Jesus would not have returned to heaven in His body, but, as the disciples hoped, He would have set up His Kingdom on the earth. What if He would have forcibly put down all rulers and set up His eternal

Kingdom? You and I would never be able to see Him...except on satellite TV.

There are over 6 billion people on the earth and most of them are more important than me. Any idea how long the line would be just to see Him, not to mention trying to get a personal audience with Him? But because Jesus went away in His body, He could return by His Spirit and *live in people!* Now anyone can have a personal audience with Him.

God's Brilliant Plan was not just to be seen by people or even to be listened to by people, but to *live in people.* The difference in the Old Covenant and the New Covenant can be clearly seen in the difference between these two words – *"on"* and *"in"*. *On* stone, *in* hearts; external (written *on* stone) or internal (written *in* our hearts).

What Is The New Covenant, Really?

Here it is – *Christ living in and through you*!

The New Covenant is *grace*, the unearned power of God living *in* and *through* us. The New Covenant is the faith of Abraham that says that God will be faithful to do for me and *in* me what I cannot do for myself. How? By living *in* and *through* me by the power of grace, which is, *"Christ in me"*!

Every time we take communion we are to remind ourselves of what He said that night around the table. Paul said *"In the same way He took the cup also after supper, saying, "This cup is the new covenant in My blood...as you do this be reminded of me"* (1 Cor. 11:25-26).

I can hear the Lord Jesus say to them and to us, *"The sacrifice of my blood and body will open a new and living way for God to live in you. This is the New Covenant your fathers looked forward to but never experienced. God, the Lawgiver and Giver of Life, will come to live in and through you. This New Covenant will be better than the Old because what was written on stone will now be living in you. The Spirit who has been with you, shall be in you. The peace I have, you will have, because I will be living in you".*

A New Covenant understanding of communion is essential. The act of taking the bread and wine *into* ourselves is to be a constant reminder of *who now lives in us.*

Listen again to Jeremiah, *"The New Covenant will not be like the Old. The Old Way was on stone but the New Way will be in people. The Old was law written on stone but the New will be the Lawgiver living in people!"*

The Lawgiver actually living *in* people? Could this be true?

Chapter Eight

On, In...
What's The Big Deal?

Is it possible that the real difference in the *Old Way* and the *New Way* is found in understanding the concept of *"on"* and *"in"*?

Is it possible that the most important difference in the Old Covenant and the New is this?

The Law written *"on"* stone or the Lawgiver living *"in"* people.

It's starting to look that way, but then I ask myself,

"What's the big deal? How important can this really be?"

The Foundation For Everything

Apparently Paul thought it was the basis of everything. In writing to the Corinthian church he describes the foundation upon which their entire life in Christ should be based.

Remember, the church in Corinth struggled with the two things you and I struggle with –

1) How can I see the fruit of the life of Christ show up in my life?

2) How can I have peace no matter how hard the circumstances?

The Corinthian church was failing in both these areas in some pretty embarrassing ways. Paul wrote to them about immorality, legal battles, demonic strongholds in their minds, intense selfishness toward each other, and many other carnal behaviors. Pretty much all the stuff God's people struggle with today.

But Paul's answer was not encouraging them to *"try harder"*. As strange as it may seem at this point in our journey, his solution was wrapped up in getting them to understand the importance of this little word – *"in"*.

Read the progression he leads them through as he tells them how to overcome their weaknesses and failures.

> *"Do you not know that you are a temple of God and that the Spirit of God dwells in you?"* (1 Cor 3:16 NAS)

After writing more about what fruit should be coming out of their lives, he asks them again –

> *"...do you not know that your body is a temple of the Holy Spirit who is in you , whom you have from God, and that you are not your own?* (1 Cor 6:19 NAS)

These questions were not designed to get them to try harder by making them ashamed. He was calling them back to what they believed in the beginning and what they must put their faith in again – *Christ living in them!*

In the second letter he makes it crystal clear that this understanding is indeed the foundation for everything.

*"Test yourselves to see if you are in the faith; examine yourselves!
Or do you not recognize this about yourselves, that Jesus Christ is
in you?"* (2 Cor 13:5 NAS)

Listen to Paul's three main points –

Test yourselves – not to see if there is sin in your life. He had
already listed many of their failures. But test yourself to where
you are putting your faith, where your confidence lies, what you
are trusting in for the power to overcome.

Examine yourselves – not to condemn yourself for where you
are falling short but to see where you are putting your confidence.
Examine what you believe about yourself and what you believe
about this *New Way* of Christ living *in* you.

Recognize this about yourselves...Jesus Christ lives in you!
This was Paul's answer for all they struggled with and all they
desired to see produced in their lives. Recognize this, put your
effort in believing this, put your confidence in the *New Way*.

I Have Been Confused About *"The Faith"*

A quick word study reveals that the New Testament writers
used the phrase *"the faith"* in a very specific way. The word
"faith" as in trust, expectation or abounding hope, is a common
word used throughout the Bible. But the phrase, *"the faith"*, is
used to describe a specific belief.

The common thinking today is that *"the faith"* means
something like "Jesus Saves", or "Christ is Lord". But Paul
defines *"the faith"* as a lifestyle of believing Christ was literally
living *in* them. *"The faith"* was the specific belief that Christ was,
in fact, living *in* them. And this radical belief set the early church
apart from all other Jews and every other religion of its day. This
belief gave them an ability to live differently than anyone else.

61

Look again at his questions to the Corinthians. *"Test yourselves...examine what you believe about yourself...are you in 'the faith'...have you stopped recognizing this about yourself, that Christ is living in you?"*

Paul clearly believed this was the solution for the dilemmas they faced.

They Meant Something Different By *"The Faith"*

Virtually every New Testament writer used this phrase, *"the faith"*, and they must have meant something different than we typically do today.

From Acts constantly referring to *"the faith"*, to the epistles talking about *"the household of the faith"*, to having *"joy in the faith"*, to *"the mystery of the faith"*, to people who *"denied the faith"*, or those who had *"gone astray from the faith"*, to Jude's admonition to *"contend for the faith that was once delivered to the saints"*. *"The faith"* was specific and clear to them; and it was the foundation of their lives.

Paul saw that the real test of our ability to live in *"the faith"* depends on how strongly we recognize that Jesus Christ *lives in us*. Not just *"believe in Jesus"*, not just *"trust in Jesus"*, but experiencing a lifestyle of constant recognition that Jesus Christ is *living in me, now!*

Paul was not talking about eternal salvation. These people were born again but they were not seeing much of the fruit of the Spirit in their lives and they had little peace in times of hardship. The key to succeeding in both of these areas was learning to live in *"the faith"* of Christ living *in* them, now!

Believing and trusting are absolutely essential, but believing and trusting in what? My ability to make and keep better promises to God; or the amazing truth that He is *alive in me*, now?

I want to learn how to trust that His life, nature, character and power are not just available to me, but already *in me*. I want to put my confidence in that one thing Paul put his confidence in. *"I am confident of this very thing, that He who began this good work in you, He will complete it!"* (Phil. 1:6)

The President Of Our Club

Until that encounter on the Damascus road, Paul had been a high achiever in the "Promise Maker's" Club. He had spent his life trying hard, doing all he knew to make the *Old Way* work. He said to the Philippian believers that if anyone had a reason to put confidence in human effort, it would be him. Listen as Paul explains all the reasons he would have to boast...if this depended on human achievement.

> *"...I could have confidence in myself if anyone could. If others have reason for confidence in their own efforts, I have even more! ...circumcised when I was eight days old...born into a pure-blooded Jewish family...of the tribe of Benjamin...a member of the Pharisees, who demand the strictest obedience to the Jewish law...zealous...I harshly persecuted the church. And I obeyed the Jewish law so carefully that I was never accused of any fault..."* (Phil.3:3-6)

By right of genetics and accomplishment, Paul was apparently the chapter president of our club. Yet he begins this passage by saying, *"We put no confidence in human effort. Instead, we boast about what Christ Jesus has done for us"*. And he ends with, *"I no longer count on my own goodness or my ability to obey God's law..."* (Phil 3:3-9 NLT).

Here is an important question. Can a Christian enjoy the eternal benefit of salvation by grace, but not enjoy the benefits of grace working in them now, producing the fruit, the nature and the peace of Jesus? *Most certainly!* In fact, it is a most common way for Christians to live. Not intentionally, but as we are coming to see, it happens because we just don't understand the *New Way.*

This *"easy and light life"* has been misrepresented to us. The master deceiver is good at his job. Though he has no new tricks, the old ones seem to keep working. And *Old Way* thinking has caused many of us to inadvertently cooperate with him.

This is a good description of me for the first thirty years of my Christian life and ministry. I truly believed my new birth was completely the work of God, a free gift that I did nothing to earn. And I began, almost immediately, trying to earn everything else by working hard in my human effort.

I have to face the hard truth about myself. I have been living in the New Covenant with regard to salvation but living in the Old Covenant in my everyday life. I have been trusting in my ability to make and keep better promises to God. But Paul clearly believed that we are to put all our trust in a present reality; *Christ living in me!*

It's starting to come clear to me that the most important little word in the Bible could really be this word *"in"*. The New Covenant seems to be all about *Him in me.* New Covenant grace really is all about Him; His Spirit, life, and power *living in me.*

A New Ability In Me

As a newly converted hippie in 1967, I quickly learned the Bible Paul carried must have been the King James Version. At least, that's what the people I met in those early days seemed to think. Many of the verses I think of today first come to mind in the KJV because that's how I first memorized them.

One of those beginning KJV memory verses is Rom 8:11, *"But if that same Spirit that raised Christ from the dead dwell in you, He shall quicken your mortal body..."*

Do you see it?

"...if that same Spirit dwell in you..." Paul's emphasis seems to clearly be on the concept of the Spirit of the resurrected Christ living *in* them.

The phrase *"quicken your mortal bodies"* literally means *"make you alive with the resurrected Christ's life in you"*. This was not some mystical concept or reassuring mental awareness. But Paul believed this was an actual fact. He clearly believed that the Spirit of the resurrected Christ was actually living in his mortal body. And he believed that would make all the difference.

Listen to the larger passage in the New Living Translation.

> *"But you are not controlled by your sinful nature. You are controlled by the Spirit if you have the Spirit of God **living in you**. (And remember that those who do not have the Spirit of Christ **living in them** are not Christians at all.) Since Christ **lives within you**, even though your body will die because of sin, your spirit is alive because you have been made right with God. The Spirit of God, who raised Jesus from the dead, **lives in you**. And just as he raised Christ from the dead, he will give life to your mortal body by this same Spirit **living within you**."* (Rom 8:9-11NLT)

Five times in this short passage Paul declares the issue was about believing Christ was actually living *in* them. The power to live under the control of the Spirit comes from recognizing He lives *in* you. The more I recognize this truth and the more I put my faith in Him living *in* me, the more I see Him living *through* me. This is true New Covenant grace, the power of the risen Christ living *in* us. This is not just a sweet, reassuring concept or mental comfort. This is a power, an ability that comes from a *"greater one"* living *in* me.

John knew that the reality of *"Christ in me"* was the foundation upon which all other truth rested. After seeing multitudes transformed by the New Covenant, he declared that the people of God could stand firm *"...because greater is He who is in you than he who is in the world."* *(1 John 4:4 NAS)* With Him living in us, we are given the greater power of His life *in* us. In the New Covenant, the Lawgiver comes to live *in* people, empowering them to live differently. John understood that the *"greater one"* living *in* us is the *source* of our ability to live differently. And until I learn to consistently put my faith in *Him living in me*, I will keep renewing my membership in the *"Promise Maker's"* Club.

Someone Else Living In Me

Many years ago in China, Watchman Nee declared in his classic, The Normal Christian Life, that Christianity is all about learning to *"live life through the power of another who lives in you"*. This is what all New Testament writers wrote about. This is what Jesus talked about around the table the night He was betrayed. This is what the early believers thought about, talked about, prayed about and worshipped about. There is a greater one living in me.

Paul boldly claims there was another life living within him, and this resulted in that *"other one"* living through him.

> *"I have been crucified with Christ; and it is no longer I who live, but Christ lives in me; and the life which I now live in the flesh I live by faith in the Son of God, who loved me and gave Himself up for me. I do not nullify the grace of God, for if righteousness comes through the Law, then Christ died needlessly."* (Gal 2:20-21 NAS)

Let me restate Paul's words as they have begun to come alive to me.

"I have been crucified with Christ, but wait a minute, I do live. But wait a minute, it's not actually me who is living, it is Christ living in me. The life I am now living in my human body I live by constantly putting my faith in Christ living through me. And I do not short circuit the power of God's grace working in me by thinking I can do this in my own power. This is why Christ died, so He could now live in and through us."

Needlepoint it on your pillow, make it the screensaver on your computer, or tattoo it on your arm! This is our *New Way* statement of faith, this is our Anchor of Hope, this is our Declaration of Dependence! There is a *"greater one"* living His life through us!

This Really Is Good News

On my journey into true grace, I am beginning to see that this is the heart of the New Covenant. This really is the *"Good News"*. If the normal Christian life is supposed to be all about learning to let Jesus live His nature and character through me, I can see how this would have tremendous impact on my struggle and frustration.

His nature and character contains all the things I want to be and all the things the Bible says I should be seeking to become. If my job in the New Covenant is to somehow learn to cooperate with Him as He lives through me, then the rules to this *New Way* really have changed. What a relief this would be.

And isn't this really the heart of what Jesus said?

"All of you who are worn out from trying to keep all the rules and worn down from trying to be good enough for God to love, come and get hooked up with me, I will give you rest. What I have for you will be easy and light because I will live it in and through you". He says my job is to get "yoked up" with Him. Then He promises His yoke will be easy on me and the only burdens He will lay on me will be light.

Inside Out or Outside In, That Is The Question

Let's go back to what Jesus said around the table that last night.

"It is to your advantage that I go away. This will allow the Spirit to come and live in you. He will be in you as the Comforter and the Teacher. He will constantly remind you of the things I have taught you. But He will do it from the inside. I am the way, the truth and the life. And this new, abundant life will be working from the inside out".

Again, I see the heart of the New Covenant. This life will come from the inside and work its way out. The *Old Way* was from the *outside in*, the *New Way* is from the *inside out*.

Every major world religion shares this same dilemma. They are each about doing certain things on the outside hoping that it will change the inside. Judaism has the Law of Moses, Islam has the Islamic Law of the Koran, Buddhism has the Eight Fold Path to Enlightenment, Hindus have karma, the law of sowing and reaping, with hundreds of variations of the same basic rules and laws.

The Eastern religions build in reincarnation because no human can ever get all the outer rules right the first time around. So you keep coming back, perhaps hundreds of times, working your way up the ladder through reincarnated attempts. In one form or another, they all share the same belief. By doing the right things outwardly you can change the inner man. Everything is based on earning god-likeness by human effort from the outside in.

But Jesus introduced a completely different plan. *"Invite me to live in you and I will bring the free gift of being made right with God. Then I will begin to work inside you, changing the nature of who you are. And as you allow me to work in you, your outside behavior will change."* *Inside out* instead of *outside in*.

68

Something is happening inside of me which results in a change in my outward behavior.

If this is true, it's more than just "good news". For a longing-to-be-former-member of the *"Promise Maker's"* Club like me, this is fantastic!

What Is This Vine/Branch/Fruit Thing All About?

It was also around the table that night where Jesus said, *"I am the vine and you are the branches. The Father's plan is that you bear much fruit. But apart from me you can nothing. Remember all the things we have talked about for the past three years, all the things you are to do and not do, be and not be, say and not say, think and not think. Listen carefully. Just hearing those things will not empower you to actually do them. Apart from me living in you, you can do none of these things, because I am the vine and you are the branches."* (John 15:1-5)

This whole **vine>branch>fruit** thing seems to have something to do with the *"source"* of my ability to bear fruit. This is clearly part of my struggle. How do I tap into the *"source"* of becoming a *"fruit-producer"*?

Chapter Nine

Whose Fruit Is This, Anyway?

"Abide in Me, and I in you. As the branch cannot bear fruit of itself unless it abides in the vine, so neither can you unless you abide in Me. I am the vine, you are the branches; he who abides in Me and I in him, he bears much fruit, for apart from Me you can do nothing." (John 15:4-5 NAS)

Remember, this is all taking place in those last few hours around the table and on the short walk to the garden. These are the last words Jesus will be able to say to His remaining eleven guys before their world falls apart. What He says here must be able to hold them while the very foundation of their belief is rocked by what will happen in the next few hours. When it looks as if all is lost, these words will have to give them real hope for their future.

"A little while and you won't see me. But a little while and you will see me again and your hearts will have a joy no man can take away. This is going to shake you, you will weep and mourn. But the end result will be that the Spirit of God will come to live in you. No matter what happens next, I will not leave you as orphans. My Father and I will come by the Spirit and live in you!" (paraphrased from John chapters 14,15,16). All of this can only be understood

in the context of Jesus saying, *"This is the* New Covenant *in my blood"*.

The *Old Way* Cannot Work

In the midst of preparing them for the shock that will be coming in a few hours, He is also laying out the game plan for how this New Covenant will be implemented. They had built a foundation on mistakenly thinking they could make the *Old Covenant* work with Jesus as the new leader. That foundational way of thinking had to be torn out. To bring them to the *New Way*, the inability of the *Old Way* had to be made crystal clear.

It is very important to see that many of the parables Jesus taught were not instructions on how to live but illustrations to show how the *Old Covenant* cannot work. Several of the parables end up sounding like you can buy or earn eternal relationship with God. Many of them seem to say you earn relationship with God by doing all the right things. But in fact, Jesus was illustrating how the *Old Covenant* never contained the means to the end they wanted, which was true relationship with God as their Father.

Many of the parables seem to be contradictory to what Paul, Peter, James, and John taught later and they can create real confusion unless we see them for what they were intended to be. Jesus was standing at the end of the *Old* and the beginning of the *New*, preparing them for what was about to come. He had to get through to them that night about the *source* of the relationship He wanted them to have with the Father.

The Issue Was *Source*

Jesus says, *"This how the New Covenant is going to work. As you abide in me and I abide in you and you will be able to draw fruit-producing life from me. My life will be in you, it will work through you and fruit will show up in your life as a result. The source of your life and the source of your fruit will be Me living in you."*

Look again at John 15:4 – *"The branch cannot produce fruit of itself"*. The branch *cannot* produce fruit *of itself!* It does not get much clearer than this. But it's taken a long time to come clear to me. On my journey I have not understood that this kind of talk was designed to help them get clear about the *source*. I kept getting frustrated about my lack of ability to produce the results. But He is talking about the *source* of the ability to produce fruit. I can now see that Jesus' words, *"of itself"*, clearly tells the disciples that they would not be the source of this fruit-producing ability.

The *source* of fruit-producing ability is not the branch. The source is not *"of itself"*. The *source* of fruit-producing ability is in the vine. That ability flows <u>*from*</u> the vine, <u>*through*</u> the branch. The result? Fruit shows up *on* the branch where everyone can see it and anyone can benefit from it.

But what is the <u>*source*</u> of that fruit-producing power?

Certainly it is not the branch. We know that. If you cut off the branch it will not continue to bear fruit. But the vine will. The vine will continue to produce more branches and they will continue to bear more fruit because the *source* of the fruit-producing power is in the vine, not in the branch.

You Cannot Do This

This is why Jesus made such a strong point of saying the Father had ordered that they bear much fruit, but they could not do it themselves. After telling them how the branch cannot bear fruit by its own effort Jesus says, *"And neither can you"*. How frustrating this is if I am depending on myself.

Listen to Jesus as He talks to them around the table.

"You must bear lots of fruit. God ordains it. God demands that you bear lots of fruit. But you can't. But you must because the Father has ordained it. But you can't because you don't have the ability within yourself. But you must."

Yikes! This is the frustrating cycle I have been in for years.

Jesus had to hit this hard because He had to break them out of the Old Covenant mentality, the *Old Way* of thinking. *"You can do nothing!"* They had to see that in the New Covenant they were not the *source*. He is the *source* and their job is to abide in Him and let Him abide in them. They were to be the *conduit* for this amazing ability.

I begin to envision the New Covenant might be something like this:

Vine > Branch > Fruit

The life is *in* the vine, it flows *through* the branch and fruit is the obvious result. The vine is the *source* of the life. The branch is the *channel* through which the life flows. The fruit is the *result* of the life coming from the source, through the branch, causing fruit to grow. This seems like it might actually be an *"easy and light"* way to produce fruit.

I don't ever remember going through an orchard and hearing grunts, groans or promises being made. When the roots go down into good soil and the branches stay attached to the vine, fruit is the natural result. *The natural result?* Yes! The natural result of roots going into good ground and life flowing through the vine into the branch will be fruit showing up in *"due season"*. Now that sounds like it could actually be an *"easy and light"* life.

What is the job of the branch in the New Covenant? Keep drawing life from the vine. Keep seeing Him as my *source*. Hang on to Him and keep letting life flow. Draw near to God and He will draw near to me. Keep drawing near to the source of life and reject anything that causes me to draw back.

Which Rose Is Dead?

I have a great friend, Arlen Blaylock, whom I have been honored to mentor as I have been traveling on this journey into true grace. Arlen is a gifted servant-leader and a very effective and wonderfully practical teacher. While teaching on this subject of the branch drawing all its life from the source, which is the vine, he shared this powerful, perspective-changing illustration. *(I really wish I could take credit for it but he will be reading this book and, though I suspect I am not always above stealing good material, I do know I don't like to get caught.)*

Arlen came into our meeting one day with two roses, one dead, dry and brown; the other a lovely red, full and beautiful. *"I cut this one a few days ago"*, he said, *"and left it in the sun on the dash of my car. The second rose I cut this morning and put it in this glass of water. Which one is dead?"* Without really thinking, we all answered, *"The brown, wilted one"*. He gave us just a moment to think through our answer and then said, *"Actually, they are both dead. The wilted one has just had a little more time for its death to show"*.

The rose has life in it only as long as it stays connected to the vine, only as long as it continues to draw its life from the vine. Once it's cut from the vine, it is dead. It's dead because the rose is not the source of its life, the vine is the source. And once it's cut from the vine, it's cut off from its source of life. It just may take a little time for the moisture to dry up and for death to show on the outside.

Grace Is Power, The New Covenant Is The Source

Remember, New Covenant grace is *"charis"*. It is all about the unearned power of His life being lived through us. The New Covenant in His blood speaks to us about the *source* of this power. His death, Paul says, made it possible for Him to live *in* us. He died that we might live. We live because He lives *in* us. Grace is the fruit-producing power of Christ's life *in* us. He is the source of all grace, all true unearned power. The New Covenant in His blood connects us with the source so true grace can work *in* us and *through* us.

Grace is unearned power. Power to do what? Power to produce the fruit, the nature, and character of the vine. Grace is the power to abide in the vine and draw life from the source.

Remember, the New Covenant is *"Christ in us"*. He is the source of the New Covenant life. *Grace* is the power of His life within us. These words are interchangeable:

The New Covenant is grace. Grace is the New Covenant.

By putting my faith in His death and resurrection, I am made right with God and He comes to live *in* me. *"Old Way"* thinking says I can do it if I just try hard enough. The *New Way* is depending fully upon Him *in* me. By denying my human ability and putting my faith in His grace, His ability comes alive within me.

My Fruit? His Fruit? I'm Confused!

I don't want to get too "spooky" for you but early in my own journey into true grace I had a weird, but wonderful experience with the Lord. I don't hold this out as an example to emulate but I am trying to honestly share what happened to me and how it affected me.

One night, after several days of corporate prayer as a church, I ended up on the floor off in a corner. It was one of those wonderful experiences where everything else seemed to fade away and I was overwhelmed by the Lord's presence. In that moment, I felt the Lord clearly say, *"Quote Gal. 5:22"*.

Later, some friends around me said they heard me say, *"Now the fruit of the Spirit is love, joy, peace, patience, kindness, goodness, gentleness, faithfulness and self-control"*. I felt the Lord say, *"Quote it again"*. So I began, *"Now the fruit of the Spirit is love, joy, peace, patience..."*. I felt the Lord stop me and say *"Again"*. So I began again, *"Now the fruit of the Spirit is..."*.

At that moment I felt I heard the Lord say, *"Stop, you don't believe this means what it says"*. I felt shocked and responded, *"I do believe it means what it says"*. *"No"*, I felt the Lord say, *"you believe it actually means 'Now the fruit of a Christian who tries really, really hard...'"*.

And suddenly I saw it.

All these years I had read, *"Now the fruit of the Spirit is..."*. But I believed *"Now the fruit of a Christian who tries really, really hard is..."*. I had been a pastor, teacher, and conference leader around the world for 30 years by that time, and I never understood whose fruit this actually is. It's the Holy Spirit's fruit. This fruit is the nature and character of Christ. His nature is love, joy, peace, patience, kindness, goodness, gentleness, faithfulness, and self-control (Gal.5:22). Those character qualities show in my life only as I allow Him to live through me.

Whose fruit is it? *It's His!* It just shows up in my life as I draw life from the *source*.

What's The Big Deal?

But you may be asking, *"What's the big deal? My fruit, His fruit, isn't the issue that we bear fruit?"* It is a big deal. In fact, it's the biggest deal because, in this issue, you cannot do the right thing in the wrong way and get any good results. There will be no fruit if we don't get this right.

Let's imagine you own an apple tree, it grows in your back yard and its roots go down deep into good soil. The fruit which the tree produces is yours. It's yours, not because you made it grow but because it grew in your yard. You can do anything you want with it. You can eat it, you can give it away or you can throw it at your neighbor's dog. You get all the benefit from it because it's yours, it grew on the tree in your yard. But you didn't have to grunt and groan to pop it out. You get the benefit but you didn't do the work.

Listen to Paul tell the Christians in Rome, *"The kingdom of God is not comprised of rules about what you eat or don't eat, drink or don't drink, but the Kingdom is made up of the righteousness, peace and joy that is found in the Holy Spirit"* (Rom. 14:17). Righteousness, peace and joy make up the nature of Jesus. The fruit of His nature is in me because His Spirit *lives in me*. The Kingdom of God is made up of what the Spirit produces in the lives of those who depend on Him.

The Holy Spirit produces His fruit. He lives in me. His fruit grows in me by His power. I get all the benefit because the fruit grows in me. I didn't do any of the work because it's His fruit not mine. But all the benefits show up in my life. And other people benefit because of what's growing in my life. When I allow Him to grow peace within me, others benefit. When I allow Him to grow faithfulness in me, others benefit. When I allow Him to grow patience in me, others benefit. Just ask my wife.

Confidence and Credit

It really does matter whose fruit this is. This is a big deal. If it's His fruit, it's His responsibility to produce it. It's my responsibility to keep drawing life from Him, to keep putting my confidence in His work in me and to keep giving Him the credit for whatever good comes out of me.

I have always thought I understood what kind of fruit I was supposed to produce as a Christian. Now I am starting to see whose fruit it actually is and where He wants it to grow.

But being a bit dull in my thinking, I foolishly say, *"This is a great deal. Now give me the rules so I can make it work!"*

Chapter Ten

The Law Was Meant To Fail

As I said earlier, I think I have done a reasonably good job over the years of teaching people *what* they are supposed to become as Christians. But I have done a very poor job of teaching people *how* to become. It is the process of *"becoming"* that causes us the most frustration.

As we address the reason the Law was meant to fail, it's important to understand what the word *"Law"* means. Remember, definition does matter.

> **Law is any rule I think I must keep so God will love me, accept me, take care of me, and allow me into His presence.**

For the Jews, it was the Law given through Moses and the *"traditions of the elders"* added later. These were viewed as the things God expected them to do in their own effort. Then, and only then, did they believe God would do anything good for them through His effort. If they failed in even one area, they were guilty of failing in all the Law. If they failed to keep the Law, then they couldn't expect God to take care of them. The obvious conclusion was to believe that every adverse circumstance was punishment or cursing from God for failing to keep the rules.

For us, our *"law"* may be certain parts of Bible verses or church traditions that we have been convinced we must do, in our own effort, before God will do anything good for us through His effort. Since human effort is doomed to fail, we then live in a cycle of what Paul called *condemnation*. Condemnation means *"a fearful expectation of judgment and punishment"*.

The result? We view every adverse circumstance as punishment from God for our failure to be perfect. Or at the very least, we expect God to remove His protection from us and let the devil take a shot at us because we are just *"getting what we deserve"*.

Pop Quiz

Here's a good test. What are the first things you think about when adverse circumstances come? *"What have I done wrong?" "I must have missed the will of God." "I knew I should have read my Bible more." "I just didn't confess the Word enough." "I have to learn to 'plead the blood' sooner (or louder)." "I am just getting what I deserve." "I knew shouldn't have eaten that breath mint during my fast. Now I am being punished for breaking the rules."*

Notice that each thought revolves around *"I"* and each thought confirms *"an expectation of judgment and punishment"*. Yet, Paul says the normal Christian life should be free from this condemnation. Could this way of thinking be linked to our misunderstanding of the true grace of God and its work in our lives? Could this be a result of misunderstanding what we are responsible for and what God has promised He will do in us?

If we misunderstand true grace, then we can't fully appreciate true mercy. If we don't understand true mercy, we can never understand what *qualifies* us for God's unconditional love and fatherly care. The result? Condemnation, regret and constantly second-guessing our decisions about the *"perfect will of God"* when circumstances seem to go against us.

We Are Looking For The Source

Remember, we are seeing that the *source* of our ability to obey Him must come from Him living *in* us. Then the results of His work will show up as the fruit of the Spirit in our lives. We are not looking for an excuse for ungodliness. We are not looking for a free pass for loose living. We are looking for the *source*, the ability that will produce true righteous behavior in our everyday lives. He is the vine, and by abiding in Him, we are assured of increasing fruit production.

Do not forget how far we have come together in this journey. We want the *"easy and light"* life Jesus promised. But we have learned that He also said the *New Way* would produce what the *Old Way* could not – *a growing ability to keep His commandments.* Could it be that while we have spent so much time and effort learning *"what"* we are supposed to become, we have been misled about *"how,"* misled about the source of the ability to become those things?

Here is a critical truth I am learning the hard way –

Knowing what you are supposed to do and become
does not give you the ability to do and become.
But it does create great frustration.

I am also learning that this often confusing, and frequently painful, frustration is a gift from God. It drives us to search for something different, something new, and to look for something that really works. This frustration with our inability is designed to drive us to Him in search of His ability. *This is the very frustration the Law was designed to produce!*

What The Law Was Designed To Do

One of the main purposes of the Law was to cause people to run out of their own ability and run to Him. God wants the law to force us into saying, *"Lord, if this is what You require, I can't do this"*. This frustration with our inability was meant to drive us to the *source* of true ability.

The Law clearly defined what it would take to live righteously before God. The Law pushes us in the direction of our only hope. And the frustration the Law produces in honest seekers is what brings us to God's goal for all life, the New Covenant in Jesus.

I know I am running the risk of gross oversimplification, but I have an excuse. I am an old hippie and a high school dropout. This has to be very simple for me to understand it. So, with apologies to my true theologian friends, I want to suggest that Paul spelled out three reasons why God gave the Law. This is not meant to be exhaustive, but an attempt to be simple and clear.

1 – The Definition

The Law was important because it clearly defined what God thinks is right and wrong. Whether they could understand all the symbols and shadows, they knew what God said about right and wrong. *"...so that through the commandment sin would become utterly sinful."* (Rom 7:13 NAS) God's people needed to know what God defined as sin. The Law clearly defines what was right and wrong in God's eyes. In the Law, some of the things the surrounding tribes thought were acceptable and normal were defined as clearly being wrong for God's people.

2 – The Tutor

Listen to Paul as he tells the Gentile believers, who had just discovered the Law, what its real purpose is. *"Therefore the Law has become our tutor to lead us to Christ..."* (Gal 3:24-25 NAS) The Law wasn't meant for them to put their faith in, but to show them how badly they needed to stay connected to the *source*. The Law's perfect standards made them feel hopeless and condemned and then led them to their only *source* of hope and freedom. It was the tutor, the schoolmaster, the teacher to lead them to the *source*, *"Christ in you, the hope of Glory"*. (Col. 1:27)

3 – The Endgame

"For Christ is the end of the law for righteousness to everyone who believes." (Rom 10:4 NAS) The end of the Law, its goal, its destination is for us to find our source in Christ. Our frustration in seeing *what* we are to become but not knowing *how* to become, is meant to drive us to the New Covenant in Christ. In Him, we find both His free gift of being made right with God, and His life *in* us empowering us to live differently.

When Paul saw that the believers in Galatia had started to settle for the Law outside, instead of the Lawgiver living inside, he asked if they had lost their minds. *"Have you lost your senses? After starting your Christian lives in the Spirit, why are you now trying to become perfect by your own human effort?"* (Gal 3:3-4 NLT) Paul warned them that their sincere efforts would not produce what they wanted. The shadow they were chasing would not give them the substance they sought.

Why would anyone settle for the shadow instead of the substance, the temporary instead of the eternal, or the external instead of the internal? Because they were being taught a lie. Sincere and probably well-intended by those who taught it, but still a lie. I, too, have believed this lie and have taught it with deep sincerity. And this lie keeps trying to infect my passionate desire to become more like Jesus and pollute the way I think about the Father's love and care for me.

This lie is meant to keep me from the *source* of all my inner man craves to become. I struggle, I fail, and sometimes I just don't want to do the godly thing. *(Please don't be shocked at my confession)* But deep inside me there is a spirit man who wants to know God and please Him. And something keeps telling me I can only accomplish this through the *New Way*. But the devil knows the best way to keep me from the *New Way* is to keep me looking to myself as the source. Do you recognize the doorway back into the *"Promise Makers"* Club?

Why The Law Must Fail To Do What We Think

When I say the Law was meant to fail, I mean God meant for it to fail to do what we mistakenly think it should do for us. The Law has always done what God intended it to do, which is drive seekers to Him. But the Law had to fail in doing what people wanted it to do for them. *"...because of its weakness and uselessness (for the Law made nothing perfect)..."* (Heb 7:18-19 NAS) The Law failed to do what the people wanted it to do, which was to make them godly through their own effort.

Rules And Regulations Within Societies

There is an important tendency in the human race that says, *"Just give me the rules and I can fix this. Show me the steps and I will work hard until I get it right".* This way of thinking is important in a fallen world for civilization to prosper and maintain some kind of peaceful co-existence.

The Bible clearly teaches us that, in order for people to live together in some basic harmony, there must be certain qualities such as diligence, order, faithfulness, integrity, a strong work ethic and, dare I say, a certain kind of *"capitalism"*. The law of sowing and reaping is essential for societies to thrive and provide peace and safety in the natural realm. Self-determination and the rewarding of hard work are critical elements God built into the natural order.

But this is not how we interact with God. Keeping His "rules" has to be the *result* of Him in us, not the *result* of our efforts. If by keeping any list of rules, *through human effort*, we could produce the righteousness and holiness of God, then we would deserve all the credit. And let's be honest. If human effort could, in fact, make us like God, He wouldn't be much of a God, would He?

God has intended for Law, or any set of religious expectations, to drive us to put our trust in Christ as our only hope. When we agree with God that our puny efforts cannot accomplish what must be accomplished, then and only then, He can live *in* and *through* us.

Our best efforts must fail. The human attempt to fully keep the law must fail.

One, so He gets all the credit.

Two, so the work done in us will not be natural, but truly *"super"* natural.

87

The result of His work in and through us will then be true *godliness,* as opposed to really good *"human-ness".*

My Best Efforts Stink

One of the verses frequently used to convince people of their need for Christ is, *"But we are all as an unclean thing, and all our righteousnesses are as filthy rags"* (Isa. 64:6 KJV). However, Isaiah's message is not to the lost but to God's people who are trusting in their own abilities. He refers to their iniquities later in the passage, but the word *"righteousnesses"* clearly refers to their attempts to produce god-like righteousness.

For years I read this passage as it is written, *"... all our righteousnesses are as filthy rags".* But I imagined it must mean *"all our* **sins** *are as filthy rags".* That made perfect sense to my Old Way thinking but that's not what it says at all. It actually says *"our righteous deeds, our very best attempts at being godly are so far below what He can produce in us that, in comparison, our results are like filthy rags".* Here is what God thinks about the inferior results of my efforts to produce god-likeness...they stink.

The Hebrew word for *"filthy rags"* means *"menstrual rags".* This would have been deeply offensive to the Jews because of the prohibitions on blood and contamination. This shows how deeply God feels about people trusting in themselves to do what only He can do in them. It deeply offends Him.

Isaiah speaks in the following verses about the solution when he says God wants to be like a potter to us as we behave like the clay. There is a secret here that we will explore in detail in a following chapter. But let's be clear; all the rules, regulations and laws of the Old Covenant were designed to get us to give up and cry out for the *New Way,* the New Covenant, the New Testament.

But wait a minute. The New Testament is filled with laws, rules and commandments, isn't it?

Chapter Eleven

Threats Or Promises? I'm Confused

The New Testament is filled with rules, instructions, and commandments. Jesus was constantly telling His men what to do and what not to do, what to think and what not to think, what to say and what not to say. But remember, He laid out the ground rules for where they would get the ability to do these things the last night around the table when He said, *"Apart from Me living in you and you drawing your life from me, you can do none of the things I have instructed you"* (John 15:5).

This statement is about *how* they will be able to obey, not *what* they are to do. This is about the source of their ability to obey rather than the specifics of the rules. He went on to say that the Spirit would be their internal Teacher and Reminder. Jesus said the one who had been *with* them would be *in* them. The promise of the New Covenant is we will have an *internal* source of power to do what the *internal* teacher will direct us to do.

Remember the meaning of the New Covenant: *what was external will be internal, what was outside will be inside.* Christ, the truth, the way, and the life, will live *in* and *through* me. What could never be accomplished from the outside in, will now be accomplished from the inside out. But this only works if I will put my faith and confidence in this *New Way* and not trust in the *Old Way*. Trusting in the *Old Way* nullifies the power of grace because it deceptively says I can accomplish god-likeness through my power; it denies that God's power is the only thing that can make men holy and puts the credit on human effort.

New Covenant *"Law"*?

But my *"Old Way thinking"* causes me to just exchange the Jewish Law for *"Christian Law"*. I find myself doing what the Galatians did. I return to the practice of being *"saved by grace but living by works"*. I truly believe that my salvation, my regeneration, was the work of God in me and nothing I could do myself. Yet, I find myself looking to my own strength to obey in my daily life. And this seems completely logical and right. Depending on which group I am associated with, I have all the right laws, rules and traditions lying alongside my partial Bible verses or *"proof texts"* to defend this way of living.

But like the old Law, when I fail to keep a part of my new Law, I feel condemned and ashamed. I feel that a holy God wouldn't want me near Him in this condition so I must somehow find a way to fix my failure. I know if I can just fix this weakness in me then I can draw near to Him again, enjoy His presence and feel His favor. *"Surely He doesn't want me near Him in my failure. If I can just get my works right, then He will welcome me near to Him."* This sounds true enough. It seems to make perfect sense.

The Same Old Lie

This logical *"truth"* is just the same old lie. And this age-old lie is designed to keep me from the *source* of the New Covenant life. It sounds right. It sounds logical. It even sounds scriptural. But it isn't. I can't really fix myself apart from His presence and His grace working in me. Oh, I can fix a few things if they fit with my basic personality. But true transformation just isn't possible through human effort.

Paul says, *"But by the grace of God I am what I am, and His grace toward me did not prove vain..."* (1 Cor 15:10 NAS). This statement is better understood as, *"By the unearned power of God working in me I have become what I have become".* Paul knew this was all about the *source* of his ability to change. It is about the *source* of our power to *"become"*.

But my *"Old Way"* thinking links my confidence with God to my ability to keep all the rules. When I am deceived about the true meaning of grace *(His power in me),* I lose all confidence when I fail. I feel I am not worthy of His help right now because I have broken the law. I knew better, but I still fell short. I don't really have the right to expect His help now, do I?

Wait a minute. We already talked about this.

Knowing *what* to do does not give me the power to *do* it.

My inability to do all the right stuff is supposed to drive me to the *source*. The *source* of my ability to obey is His *grace* working in me. And *grace* is a free gift. I have to keep trusting in Him so His *grace* can freely flow through me. Could this be what Jesus meant when He talked around the table that night about the importance of learning to *"abide in Him"*?

Remember Paul's strong declaration of what the Christian life really is –

> *"I have died with Christ. But wait a minute, I do live. But wait a minute, it's not really me who lives. It is Christ who is living in and through me!"* (Gal. 2:20)

This is where I must put my confidence, my hope and my faith.

There Is Another Commandment

Any New Testament verse quickly becomes lifeless law if I look to myself for the power to keep it. When I make God's love conditional on my ability to obey in any given situation, I turn the writings of the New Testament into the *"letter of the law"*. Paul said the *"letter kills"* but the *"Spirit gives life"*. He is again referring to the *source*. Rules kill hope and confidence because they demand more than they enable us to produce. But the Spirit not only speaks to us inwardly about what would be pleasing to the Lord, but He *empowers* us from within to do that very thing.

Remember, this is His fruit. It's being produced *through* me, not *by* me. So each time I fail to produce the fruit of one of His commandments, I then must obey another commandment.

> *"If we say that we have no sin, we are deceiving ourselves and the truth is not in us. If we confess our sins, He is faithful and righteous to forgive us our sins and to cleanse us from all unrighteousness"* (1 John 1:8-9 NAS). If I believe this commandment then I will run to Him when I break any other commandments!

We draw near to Him for both *forgiveness* and *cleansing*. *Forgiveness* comes out of His mercy but the *power to cleanse* comes from His grace at work in us. I must learn to obey John's commandment whenever I fail to keep any other commandment.

94

But what about all those other New Testament rules and regulations?

In fact, all the New Testament instructions are given so we will know:

1)   what to draw near to Him for,
2)   what fruit to depend on Him for,
3)   what to confess as our weaknesses so His strength can work through us, and;
4)   what results we can expect to see as He does work through us.

When we see the New Testament in this light, we know what to expect and what to confess. Confessing becomes a joy rather than a terror. The *Old Way* says when I fail to keep a commandment I am guilty of not doing something I should have been able to do. I can now expect God's displeasure, anger, even punishment because God expected me to be able to do it.

But the *New Way* tells me that my failure is a clear indication I was trusting in my ability instead of His. I confess that I sinned because I was leaning on my thinking and my strength. I was trusting in myself. I confess not only the sin of what I did but also my sin of unbelief. I was not believing in the power of His life in me.

My sin is evidence that I am putting my confidence in myself. Rather than condemning me, it drives me back to believing in His grace, since it is again clear that I cannot do this on my own. My confession brings forgiveness and cleansing. It reconnects me with His grace. When I understand the *New Way*, my fellowship is not broken because of my sin. It is only broken when I refuse to confess. The goal? Become a *quicker confessor* so I can put my confidence back in the reality of Him living in me!

Are They Rules Or Promises?

*"...He is also the mediator of a better covenant, which has been enacted on **better promises**"* (Heb.8:7-8 NAS).

The Old Covenant was made of rules that couldn't empower people. So it left them feeling hopeless and condemned. They knew *what* to do but not *how* to do it. The New Covenant is made of *better promises*. These promises are about being empowered by a greater life living *in* us. Remember what Jesus told them that night, *"The Spirit will come and He will live My life through you."* As a former member of the *"Promise Makers"* Club this is exciting news. *(Notice the words "former member"? I am making progress...by faith!)*

Could this really be, not about my promises to Him, but about His promises to me? I suspect He can do a much better job of keeping His promises than I can. *Better Promises* and a better *Promise Keeper* living in me? This is a great deal!

Better Promises Produce A Better Hope

"For, on the one hand, there is a setting aside of a former commandment because of its weakness and uselessness (for the Law made nothing perfect), and on the other hand there is a bringing in of a <u>better hope</u>, through which we draw near to God." (Heb 7:18-19 NAS).

The *"former commandment"* was *"weak and useless"* because it couldn't empower people to do it. The Law just could not produce what it seemed to promise. But Jesus brought a *"better hope"*. *Him in us!* The Lawgiver living within people, teaching them what to do and empowering them to do it. This is indeed a better hope.

This is what Paul was talking about in the famous *"fear and trembling"* verse. This is one of many places where knowing only part of a Bible verse fits right into the devil's plan to deceive us about the true meaning of grace. I have traveled around the world and asked people to finish this Bible passage.

I begin quoting Phil.2:12-13, *"So then, my beloved, just as you have always obeyed, not as in my presence only, but now much more in my absence..."*. So far almost no one knows the reference. Then I quote, *"...work out your own salvation with..."* I stop here and nearly everyone finishes the verse, *"**WITH FEAR AND TREMBLING!**"* It seems everyone who has ever even driven by a church knows the *"fear and trembling"* verse. The verse doesn't end there, but few people know the rest of Paul's statement.

The next word is *"for"*. Or in modern English we would say *"because"*. This is a very important word. If I were to say to you, *"You need to turn off the electricity because..."* you would want me to finish the sentence before you did anything. Anything! Or if I were to say, *"Whatever you do, don't open the basement door because..."* you would probably want to hear the rest of that thought before you decided if you wanted to stay alone, at night, in my house.

"For" or *"because"* are words that connect one thought with the following thought. You can't understand what was just said until you connect it with the remainder of the sentence. Words like *"and, however, therefore, in addition to, or because"* are essential for us to understand the meaning. Yet few people know what follows *"fear and trembling"*.

There Is A Better Hope

Here is the rest of Paul's thought.

> *"...for it is God who is at work in you,* **both** *to will and to work for His good pleasure."* (Phil. 2:13 NAS)

Listen to it in the New Living Translation.

> *"For God is working in you, giving you the* **desire** *to obey him and the* **power** *to do what pleases him."*

What was Paul's real point? God is doing two things in you. He is giving you the *desire* to obey Him and He is giving you the *power* to obey Him. And if you try to accomplish this any other way, you better fear and tremble because you are doomed to fail. There is no other way. There is no Plan B. You work out your own salvation only by a constant revelation that it is Him working in you. Now that is, indeed, a better hope than trusting in myself!

He Is The Source Of Both Things

Do you desire to obey the Lord? That is important, it is critical, it is essential, but you can't take any credit for it. He gave you that desire. Deep within you, do you really *want* to obey the Lord? He gives that to you. He is the source of it. He is at work in you doing two things: giving you a *desire to obey* and giving you the *power to obey*. He is the source of both of these essential things. The two things we crave the most, to want to obey Him and to have the ability to obey Him? *He is the source of both things!*

Jesus said the same thing sitting around the table in that rented upstairs banquet room. *"When the Spirit comes into you, He will teach you what to do <u>and</u> give you the power to do it."* This is the New Covenant. This is the better promise and the better hope.

Paul put his faith in this better promise and lived through intense suffering because of this better hope. His confidence was in the work God was doing in him. As a top Pharisee, he knew the futility of trying to do this in his own effort. Paul drew near to God as the source of both the *desire* and the *ability*. Remember Paul's declaration, *"I am confident of this very thing, that He who began this good work in you, He will complete it!"*

I think I am beginning to understand what the New Covenant really is. I am beginning to see that grace is really about both the power to obey and tapping into the source of that power.

So, I think I am starting to understand *what* it is, but *how* do I get it to work?

Chapter Twelve

I Think I Know "What",
But How?

Why Law Can't Empower Us

The Law, God's expectations written on stone and rules written on scrolls, was impossible for humans to fully keep. Each type of human personality could do a reasonable job of keeping some of the expectations, but no one could keep them all. To keep them all would mean we were completely like God. Our inability to be completely like God is why God gave such an elaborate system of sacrifices. That system of sacrifices was to cover all the parts of the Law humans could not keep in their own power because they were...well...human.

In essence, the Law is God saying, *"If you are going to be in right relationship with Me, you must be like Me. To be like me, you must keep every legal, practical and symbolic rule I write down."* The problem is clear. How could fallen humans become like the infinitely holy and perfectly righteous God? They can't. It's just not possible. So He gave a very detailed system of sacrifices to cover the failure of weak people. The weakness of the Law was that it depended on the ability of the people to be perfectly like God.

> *"For what the Law could not do, weak as it was through the flesh (human effort), God did: sending His own Son in the likeness of sinful flesh and as an offering for sin, He condemned sin in the flesh, so that the requirement of the Law might be fulfilled in us..."* (Rom 8:3-4 NAS)

Rules Don't Work Because They Depend On Us

This is amazing in its ramifications. The Law couldn't work because it depended on human effort. *The Law couldn't work because it depended on us.* But what the Law couldn't do, God did through His Son who lives in us. Listen to it again. *"What the Law couldn't do...God did!"* What depended on us couldn't work. But what depends on Jesus works!

Look at the last part of that passage. God did it this way *"...so that the requirement of the Law could be fulfilled in us!"* If the requirement to be like God couldn't work because it depended on our effort, and He now lives in us, then the fulfillment now depends on our trusting in His effort within us.

The *Old Way* tells us *"what"*– *"become more like God"*. But the *New Way* tells us *"how"*– *"by the Spirit living His life through you"*. Remember Paul saying to the Philippians, *"I put no confidence in my human ability to obey...I am confident in this one thing, that He who began this work in me, He will complete it!"* (Phil. 3:3, 1:6)

I have been putting my confidence in the wrong thing. No wonder my faith exercises haven't worked. I have been putting my faith in the wrong person. I have been putting my hope in me and my ability, instead of Him and His ability in me. That's it! I am tearing up my membership card to the *"Promise Makers"* Club!

True Grace Is The Answer to "How"

Paul warned the Galatians to never put their confidence in their ability to keep the Law because it didn't work. It seemed to promise something it could never produce. The Law couldn't work because it only laid out the *"what"* to be. It could not give them the *"how"* to become. It laid out what the expectations were, but it couldn't give them the ability or the power to produce the expected results. It explained the *"what"* but could not produce the *"how"*. Paul's answer for them was to return to the simplicity of grace which he defined as the *"unearned power of Christ's life living through them"*.

God's brilliant plan was to put the "how" inside us.

**He puts the source of obedience within us,
The Spirit of Grace.**

This was prophesied by many of the prophets, though they could not comprehend how it could happen. We have already seen how Jeremiah prophesied about the New Covenant God planned to fulfill by putting His ability, His Spirit, Himself within us. Ezekiel, also, described this new ability that would come with the New Covenant even though he could not have understood how this would actually work.

"Moreover, I will give you a new heart and put a <u>new spirit within you</u>; and I will remove the heart of stone from your flesh and give you a heart of flesh. I will put <u>My Spirit within you</u> and

cause you to walk in My statutes, and you will be careful to observe My ordinances". (Ezek. 36:26-27 NAS)

What is God's brilliant plan?

"I will put a new spirit in you...I will put My Spirit in you..."

What is the result of God putting His Spirit in people?

"...and I will cause you to walk in My statutes".

The word *"cause"* here means to *"enable or empower"*. Once again we see the promise of the *New Way* explained in Old Testament prophesy. God wants to *enable* us to obey Him. He wants to *empower* us to live a life pleasing to Him. He does this by putting His Spirit within us. This is the work of true grace in our lives.

Look at the last part of this New Covenant promise: *"...and you will be careful to observe My ordinances."* Old Way thinking reads it like this – *"you better keep My ordinances"*. But *New Way* thinking declares it like this – *"you will be enabled to keep my ordinances, you will be empowered to keep my expectations"*.

The *"what"* is – *"keep My statutes"*. The *"how"* is – *"I will put a new spirit in you"*. The *"what"* is – *"...be careful to observe my ordinances"*. The *"how"* is – *"I will put My Spirit in you"*.

The New Covenant ability to obey is the result of His Spirit living in us. This is true grace. Our job is to keep putting our faith in believing He is, indeed, at work in us. This is the grace Paul, Peter, James and John were so excited about. This is what they described as the Good News. This is what they fought to put their faith in, and this is *"the faith that was once delivered to the saints"*. This is the *New Way*.

Beginning At The Wrong Place

Old Way thinking always begins with what you must do. It sounds very logical and scriptural to say *"If you will do this, then God will do this."* And there are plenty of partial verses or verses taken out of context to re-enforce this way of thinking. The problem is, if I begin at the wrong starting point, the right directions will lead me to the wrong destination. There is nothing wrong with the directions. So what's wrong? I started at the wrong place.

I want you to come to my house for the first time. I tell you to start driving north for two blocks, turn left and go 1.3 miles, turn right at the light and go to the second house. Those are the right directions. But if you begin on Elm Street when I thought you were starting on Main Street you will end up in the wrong place and the people living there will wonder who you are. There wasn't anything wrong with the directions. The starting place was wrong.

When we begin by believing God is expecting us to produce godliness in our own ability first, the Biblical directions will drive us to the wrong place. The right beginning place is – *"Apart from Me living in you and through you, you can't do anything!"*

The Starting Point Has Always Been The Same

This has been *God's Brilliant Plan* from the beginning. Jeremiah told us. Ezekiel told us. Even Moses told us this before any of the other prophets. Before he leaves the people, Moses reminds them where they have come from, how God has led them and what God expects from them. The *Old Way* thinking will cause us to begin reading here –

"Then the LORD your God will prosper you abundantly in all the work of your hand, in the offspring of your body and in the

> *offspring of your cattle and in the produce of your ground, for the*
> *LORD will again rejoice over you for good, just as He rejoiced*
> *over your fathers; if you obey the LORD your God to keep His*
> *commandments and His statutes which are written in this book of*
> *the law, if you turn to the LORD your God with all your heart and*
> *soul.*" (Deut 30:9-10 NAS)

We all want God to prosper us in what we do, and here is the promise that He will. But if we begin reading at this point in Deut. 30, we will believe all this begins with us doing all the right things, and until we do all the right things the right way we cannot expect God to do anything for us.

Old Way thinking will cause me to focus on the word *"IF"*. These wonderful things will happen *"IF"* I obey in everything, in all ways, in all commandments, in all statutes. It seems clear. It seems logical. So I use this passage to reinforce my *Old Way* thinking. God is waiting on me to get all this obedience worked out perfectly. This all depends on me.

Of course, if I fail in any way (and I will) my confidence is stolen, I feel condemned and I expect punishment instead of help. But I have started at the wrong beginning point. Obedience is important. But it is the goal, not the beginning.

Begin At The Beginning

What we read in Deut. 30:9-10 is the *"what"*, not the *"how"*. *How* this is going to be accomplished in us is explained by reading the earlier verses. The context here is absolutely essential. If we back up three verses, we read that God wants to do something in us *first*. And what He wants to do in us will enable us to do something as a *result*.

Verse 6 says *"Moreover the LORD your God will circumcise your heart and the heart of your descendants, to love the LORD your God with all your heart and with all your soul, so that you may live."* Verse 8 says *"...and you shall obey the Lord..."*

Do you see it? God wants to do something in us first. He wants to *"circumcise your heart".* The result of this *"circumcising"* of our hearts will be an enablement. And what will this work of God in us enable us to do? *"To love the Lord God with all our heart and soul"* and *"you shall obey the Lord".*

There it is. This is the *New Way* promise in the heart of the Old Covenant. God will do something in us that will enable us to do what our inner man craves to do; love Him with everything within us and learn to obey Him. This ability to truly love God and to grow in obedience is the *result* of a work God wants to do in us first.

Can this be true? Can my ability to love Him and do good works really be the result of Him doing a *work* in me first? Is it possible that this is what Paul was talking about when he said *"He who began a good work in you, He will complete it"*?

I am, once again, confused. Who is the Worker, what is the work and who is getting worked on?!

God's Brilliant Plan

Chapter Thirteen

Relieved To Be Just
A Lump Of Clay

On my journey into understanding God's true grace, I have come to believe that the two most important questions I must answer are:

1)   What is God really like?

2)   How does He really feel about me?

Until I understand what God is really like and how He really feels about me, I can never act like the son He wants me to be to Him. And He can never be the Father He longs to be to me. I can never trust in the power of His grace at work in me until I understand how He feels about me, now, in my struggle. Understanding what God is really like, and how He really feels about me, will tell me how He will react to my failures. Until I am sure of how He will react to my failure, I will never be able to freely confess and draw near to Him for help when I fail.

Jeremiah's Trip To The Potter's House

Jeremiah had an amazingly simple experience that speaks volumes about what God is really like and how He feels about us.

> *"The LORD gave another message to Jeremiah. He said, "Go down to the shop where clay pots and jars are made. I will speak to you while you are there." So I did as he told me and found the potter working at his wheel. But the jar he was making did not turn out as he had hoped, so the potter squashed the jar into a lump of clay and started again. Then the LORD gave me this message: "O Israel, can I not do to you as this potter has done to his clay? As the clay is in the potter's hand, so are you in my hand."* (Jer. 18:1-7 NLT)

Imagine this scene as it unfolds for Jeremiah. God says to go down to a potter's house and watch...just watch. And in watching, God is going to tell Jeremiah something very important about Himself and how He feels about the people. Remember God's words were *"Can't I be to you as this potter is to the clay?"* The relationship of the potter to the clay must say something very important about God's relationship with us.

It is critical that we understand several things about this illustrated sermon Jeremiah saw.

1)   The potter has specific plans for the clay.

2)   The potter has definite feelings about the clay.

3)   The potter has a certain reaction to the clay.

4)   The potter is actually doing the work on the clay.

The Potter's Plan – Something Useful and Valuable

The potter's plan for the clay was to take something that, in its original state, was useless and valueless. Through the work the potter was going to do, this useless and valueless lump of clay would become *useful* and *valuable*. Through the work the potter would do on and in the clay, the clay would become something that could do good work...but only as a *result* of what the potter did to it. The good work of the potter would produce an ability in the clay to do good work...but only as a *result* of the work the potter did to it.

Do you see it?

The usefulness of the clay is the *result* of the work of the potter. The clay cannot take any credit for its usefulness. It is the *result* of the potter's work.

Doesn't this sound like the New Covenant? Take something that, in its original state, is useless and valueless and work on it until it becomes useful and valuable? Doesn't this sound like the work of true grace in a human being? Remember Paul saying, *"I have become what I have become through God's grace working in me"* (1 Cor. 15:10). To put it another way, *"Any good thing in me is the result of God's grace working in me".*

How The Potter Feels About The Clay

Where did the potter get this lump of clay? He couldn't go to the craft store and get a nice, clean, pure package of modeling clay. He had to go into the countryside and find it. He had to scoop it out of the hillside and bring it home. And whatever was in the clay when he scooped it out came home with it.

When he got it home, was he under any illusions that it was clean and pure? No, he knew it was full of *"gunk"*. *"Gunk"* may be an obscure Hebrew word for rocks, twigs, leaves, bugs and all the other stuff you would find if you scooped up a bucket of dirt.

The raw material was filled with gunk. Just like you and me. The potter knew exactly what he was getting, and he brought the clay home anyway. This was part of his plan for the clay. He sees the useful and valuable future this raw material has within itself. It just needs the work of the potter to bring it out.

Remember, this is an important part of the answer to the question, "How does He really feel about me?"

Was God under any illusions about what He was getting when He called us to Himself? No, He knew everything about us. He knew exactly what He was getting in our past, present and future. David said, before he was ever born, God knew all his days and knew his every word before he ever spoke one. Now that's a scary thought. And yet, just like the potter, He scoops us up and takes us to His workshop because He has a plan for us. Because He sees a valuable future within us that just needs the work of the Potter to bring it out. Just like the potter, He is the worker and we are, and keep becoming, the *result* of His working.

The potter does not expect the clay to do any work. The potter knows he is the worker and the clay will show the *result* of his work. All the potter expects from the clay is to submit to the process.

The Handling Process

There are so many wonderful symbols we can draw from the process of the potter's work. But it all seems to come down to one basic activity. ***The potter handles the clay.*** He works the clay with his hands. He mixes in water until the clay is just the right consistency. He does this with his hands. He pokes and prods. He slaps it down on the wheel. He squeezes, he stretches and he spins it around. And all the while, his hands are feeling for something. What's he feeling for? The impurities, he's feeling for the *gunk*. He is feeling for the *stuff* he knows is in there. He knew the *gunk* was there when he dug it out and brought it home. And he still brought it home. Does this say something about how God feels about you and me?

Is the potter surprised when he finds impurities in the clay?

Of course not, he knew they were there.

Is he shocked?

Of course not, he fully expected to find them.

Is he embarrassed about the impurities he finds?

Of course not, he knew what he was getting and he chose this specific clay anyway.

Does he get angry with the clay because of the impurities he finds?

Of course not, this is completely normal. This is just what he expected. And he knows what he is going to do about them.

Remember, God is trying to tell us how He feels about us.

He says, *"I am the potter and you are the clay"*.

But *Old Way* thinking tells me God is disappointed when weakness shows up in me. It tells me God is embarrassed of me when I sin. It tells me God is angry with me because I should have known better. It tells me I have no right to worship and fellowship Him until I cleanse myself of all the impurities I have allowed to remain within me.

Old Way thinking tries to convince me God is saying, *"Get off this wheel. Get back on that shelf. I can't work with something as unclean as you. You have no business being here until you get this junk out of your life. Once you have gotten serious about being a Christian and have sanctified yourself, then I will consider working with you again!"*

How Can It Be Wrong When It Sounds So Right?

This sounds so logical. It sounds so right. It sounds so Biblical. But it's not. God said it is not. He told Jeremiah that He is just like the potter. And what does the potter do when he uncovers gunk in the clay? Does he get surprised, embarrassed, or angry? No. *He removes it!* Who does the work of removing the gunk? *The potter, not the clay.*

I know this analogy is not perfect. The clay has no free will, and we do. Because of our free will, we can do something the clay can't do. We can choose what to do. So let's give the clay its own free will. Now what is the clay's job? Cleanse itself? No. Just choose to stay on the wheel. Choose to let the potter continue to handle it. Choose to let the potter do what the potter does best.

In fact, the clay could reasonably argue that the reason the gunk was exposed was because the potter kept handling it. If the gunk bothers the potter so much then he should just stop poking around and the impurities won't get exposed and they won't be a problem. Ah, but they will.

Why Impurities Must Be Removed

The reality is some impurities are harmful to the clay. Some are more than harmful, some are deadly. If the potter leaves certain impurities in the clay, molds it to the desired shape, puts it in the kiln and fires it, wherever there is an impurity, there will be a weakness. You won't see it and you won't know it. Everything will probably look fine on the outside. Until you begin to use it. The pressure of using the pot will eventually cause the weakness to give way and the pot will be broken. Once fire-dried clay is broken, it can never be molded again. It will once again become *useless* and *valueless*.

It is in the "using" that the pressure comes.

The goal of the potter is make something useful and valuable. But he understands that the very act of using the vessel creates pressure. If the pot is just going to sit on the shelf and look pretty then it's not a big deal. But if the potter is going to use this vessel to do work, to do something of value, then it has to be able to stand the pressure.

Could this explain why we have seen so many national Christian figures being used by God and then a weakness is suddenly exposed and lives are broken? Could it be there was a serious impurity there all along that never got dealt with? Could it be that the pressure that naturally comes from being used as a vessel in the Kingdom caused the weakness to give way?

This idea of being *"used by God"* is not just in the glittering things we see on the national stage. It is much more importantly seen in the everyday life of being a godly mother, father, employee, friend and the many other ways we function as a container of God's glory and expression to the world. This is where the pressure gets intense and the battle rages strong. This is where we represent Him as He lives through us and makes us salt and light. This is where we must be able, by His grace within us, to withstand the pressure.

Why Would We Not Want To Be Handled?

Why would we not allow the potter to handle us and consistently remove the impurities? One primary reason is because *Old Way* thinking has misled us about *"What God is really like"* and *"How He really feels about us"*.

God is more often painted as the Judge who is looking for a reason to punish, rather than a Father who is looking for a way to help. He is portrayed as our Prosecutor rather than our Perfecter, our Accuser rather than our Advocate. The *New Way* warns us that we do have an accuser...but it is not God!

Condemnation should have no place in our lives, yet it is the most common feeling experienced when believers fail. Condemnation is *"the expectation of judgment or punishment"*. If I am convinced I will be punished for my impurities, I will not run to the potter to be handled. I will draw back and try to fix this myself. But the Good News is God wants to be to us as a potter is to the clay. There is no judgment, no anger and no condemnation on the potter's wheel.

In the relationship of a potter to the clay, the most natural thing in the world should be the exposure of impurities and the potter doing the work to remove them. Knowing the benefit that comes from letting the potter do his work, we should welcome it. I admit this is a complete reversal of what I have thought for many years.

The idea that God wants me to run to Him in my failure is foreign to my *Old Way* thinking. I am much more comfortable thinking God wants me to bathe before I approach Him. And I have Old Testament verses to back up that way of thinking. But the *New Way* is…well…new!

Could this be part of the *"easy and light life"* Jesus talked about? The potter handles us, exposes an impurity, we confess it and submit to his cleansing work to remove it. Doesn't this sound like John talking, *"If we confess our sins, He is faithful and just to forgive us and to cleanse us from all unrighteousness"* (1 John 1:9). No anger, accusation, or punishment. Just a faithful, loving God who wants to keep cleansing us.

There Is An Important Difference

If this is true, this takes a huge load off of me. I feel relieved to know all I have to be is a lump of clay in the potter's hands. But all analogies, all symbols and all parables break down when taken to an extreme. We are *"like"* clay but we are also very different from clay.

Once clay has been shaped and dried it can never be reworked again. Once it breaks it can never be molded again. But you and I are being handled, shaped and used all at the same time. We are being used by God in some areas while being handled and shaped in others. We sometimes have impurities exposed right while we are being used by Him. And the experience sometimes breaks us. But He can make us pliable again.

But it is not impurity that disqualifies the clay from being used. If it was, no one could ever be used by God to accomplish His purpose. Abraham, Jacob, Moses, David, Peter and nearly every hero of faith listed in Hebrews 11 would have been disqualified.

So What Does Disqualify The Clay?

If the comparison of Jeremiah 18 holds true, what disqualifies the clay? Clearly not just the presence of impurities. The exposure and removal of impurities is portrayed as a normal part of the potter's work.

Struggling with weaknesses seems to have been very normal for the early believers. In the middle of his letter to the Philippians, Paul stops and says, *"Now don't think that I have attained to all this I am writing about or that I have become perfect because I haven't"* (Phil.3:12). In Romans 7 he talked about what we all can relate to when he said, *"I sometimes do the things I know I shouldn't and I sometimes don't do the things I know I should. And sometimes I just don't understand myself"*. James 3:2 says *"For we all stumble in many ways"*. John says *"If we say we don't sin then we are liars"* (1 John 1:8).

These men understood weakness, but they also seemed to fully understand how the Heavenly Potter felt about them and their weaknesses. Their writings made it clear that He doesn't excuse impurities, but as long as we allow Him, He will constantly handle us, exposing and removing impurities within us. And this is supposed to be the *"normal Christian life"*.

So what disqualifies the clay?

Getting off the wheel! Refusing to be handled by the potter! Refusing to acknowledge the impurities for what they are; sin, failure, trusting myself rather than trusting His grace, trusting my opinion and my understanding rather than God's. If, because of arrogance or anger or fear, the clay gets off the wheel and refuses to be handled by the potter, the clay is no longer usable. And until

I climb back on that wheel in transparency, humility and confession, the potter waits.

Staying Small

Saul was chosen by God to lead Israel, but he came to a place where his heart was so hardened that the Potter could no longer handle him. He refused to get back on the wheel. Samuel described his downfall by saying, *"When you were small in your own eyes you listened to the Lord your God"* (1 Sam. 15:17). Saul's desire to be molded by God was overrun by his pride and self-defense. He no longer saw himself as *"small in his own eyes"*.

This is a great definition of Biblical humility. Humility is not thinking I am *"a worm"*, completely worthless and full of shame. I am a child of God, bought with the most precious price and Jesus took all my shame to the cross. Humility is choosing to be *"unpretentious"*, choosing to be transparent, choosing to stay small so He can be large within me. The Holy Spirit wants to help me become fully dependent on the potter to do the work of exposing and cleansing. And instead of fighting against this process, He wants to help me learn to love it. Humility is truly seeing my role in this process and constantly offering myself to the potter for *"handling"*.

This story about the potter and the clay is a really nice story. But is this theologically accurate? Is this really the way the New Covenant works? Or I am just falling right back into the same confusion I have been in for years?

Who really is supposed to be doing the work here?

God's Brilliant Plan

Chapter Fourteen

Who Is Doing The Work Here?

We have discovered that a key truth on our journey into this *"easy and light"* life is Eph. 2:8-9. *"For by grace you have been saved through faith; and that not of yourselves, it is the gift of God; not as a result of works, so that no one may boast."* (NAS)

Let me restate this truth.

"You have been saved as a result of the unearned power of God that is at work in you and this power works as you put your faith in His ability instead of yours. This power is a free gift from God so no man can take the credit for the transformation it produces within you."

Clearly, this passage is all about:

1) The **work** that is being done
2) **In whom** the work is being done
3) **Who** is actually doing the **work**
4) Where I must learn to put my **faith**

One common mistake is to think this only refers to eternal salvation and that, somehow, the results in our everyday lives depend on us. But the very next verse says, *"For we are His workmanship*, created in Christ Jesus for good works, which God prepared beforehand so that we would walk in them" (Eph. 2:10 NAS). Do you see the connection between the good works we are created to produce here and now, and the fact that we are His workmanship, reflecting the result of His work?

We Are His Workmanship

If I am His workmanship, I cannot be the "*worker*". All this time I have looked at the good works that are supposed to be produced in my life as if they were supposed to be the result of my hard work. I saw myself as the worker. But Paul says *God is the worker* and *we are the workmanship*.

The workmanship is the <u>result</u> of the worker's work.

I am writing this book on a laptop computer. It is a marvelous and mysterious piece of work. Mysterious to me, at least, because I don't have a clue as to how it works. But I do know this. It did not make itself. It is the result of a worker. Not once in the months I have been using it to write this book has it ever said, *"Didn't I do a good job of making myself?"*

What a bizarre thought. Of course it didn't make itself. It is the *result* of a worker. It is the *workmanship*. No one would ever think it made itself; even if it could somehow speak up and make that claim. And yet, I have read these verses for years and still thought I was supposed to somehow make myself into Christ's image.

My confusion takes me back to the potter's house and drives me to ask again:

1)   Who is the worker?

2)   Who is the work?

3)   What should be the results of that work?

Eph. 2:10 tells us the same thing Jeremiah learned at the potter's house. It clearly states that we will produce good works. In fact, the passage says God pre-ordained the good works you and I would produce before we were ever born. But these good works are going to be the *result* of His effort, His work, His "*handling*" of the clay.

The *result* of the potter's work is that the clay will be enabled to do good works. The clay (us) will become something useful and valuable. But this value will be a *result* of the work of the potter (God).

And the clay must never get the roles reversed. If it does, it is doomed to frustration, failure and condemnation. That describes my life for many years.

Remember Jesus saying the key to the *easy* and *light* life is to get yoked up with Him? He does the work. We walk with Him but He does the work. And He talks about the people (us) who get the roles reversed.

> "*If you are worn down and worn out from trying so hard to do it all, come to Me, learn about Me and I will give you rest. Get yoked up with Me because my yoke is easy and my burden is light. The result? You will find rest for your weary souls. You will do the work but it will be with Me carrying the heavy load.*" (Matt. 11:29-30)

The Danger of Role Reversal

Paul clearly understood his role in this process and desperately wanted us to understand it, too. *"For I am confident of this very thing, that He who began a good work in you will perfect it until the day of Christ Jesus"* (Phil 1:6-7 NAS).

Who is the worker?

God is the worker.

Who is the workmanship, the <u>result</u> of the work being done?

We are, if we put our faith and confidence in His work!

Even Isaiah understood this concept, though he could not understand the ramifications of how this would play out in the coming New Covenant. Right after he laments the inability of the people to produce any real righteousness by their feeble human efforts, he speaks out of a divine revelation and says, *"We are the clay, and You are the potter; And all of us are the <u>work</u> of Your hand"* (Isa. 64:8 NAS).

Somehow, prophetically, Isaiah caught a glimpse of this *Brilliant Plan*. *"...all of us are the <u>work</u> of Your hand"*. We are His workmanship, the *result* of His work in the human heart, personality and nature.

Western Christianity seems to be mired in this dangerous *role reversal*. You see it in the weary, worn out believers who desperately want to have peace with God, but are convinced God is waiting on them to produce Christ-like character. And we seem to be riddled with the fear that He is angry with us for any part of our lives in which we are not yet perfectly like His Son. So few sincere believers are able to truly enjoy the progress they have made because the accuser keeps them worrying about the areas they have yet to conquer. This is why our club, the *"Promise Makers"*, has such a huge membership...and it's growing!

Some of the most emotionally moving sermons I have ever heard were based on the faulty belief that God's expectation of us is to *"work harder"*. This is based on the mistaken notion that we are the workers. Some of the most powerful sermons I have ever preached were based in this same error.

It just seems so right, so logical, so scriptural. But it's not. It is a masterful deception designed by our adversary to keep us frustrated, fearful and worn-out. And most importantly, he wants us to keep putting our faith and hope in the wrong person.

I am learning what Paul seems to have clearly known. I cannot put my faith in my ability and His ability at the same time. These two things are mutually exclusive. Remember Paul said he refused to nullify the grace of God by making the mistake of putting confidence in himself as the worker.

Disconnected From The Source

This role-reversal keeps us disconnected from the power of true grace. It keeps us looking to the *wrong source*. If I am the worker, the one who is supposed to produce godliness, then I keep looking to myself and wondering what's wrong with me. It becomes easy to believe that God is mad, that He is worn out by my unwillingness and weak effort. But if He is the *worker* and if I am His *workmanship*, then I must learn to put my faith in something other than myself and my best efforts. The one thing I want to learn to believe is that *"He who began a good work in me, He will complete it"*.

My faith and confidence in God's way for living this new life connects me to the source. I have to see it the way He planned it to operate. The good works in my life must be the *result* of His working in me. Let's go back to Paul telling one of his sons in the faith, Titus, how to teach the people.

> *"But when the kindness of God our Savior and His love for mankind appeared, He saved us, not on the basis of deeds which we have done in righteousness, but according to His mercy, by the washing of <u>regeneration</u> and <u>renewing</u> by the Holy Spirit, <u>whom</u> He poured out upon us richly through Jesus Christ our Savior, so that being justified by His grace we would be made heirs according to the hope of eternal life. This is a trustworthy statement; and concerning these things I want you to speak confidently, <u>so that</u> those who have believed God will be careful to engage in good deeds."* (Titus 3:4-8 NAS)

The words *"so that"* in the above passage are very important. Those words tell us we must connect what we just read with what we are getting ready to read if we are to understand what God is saying. They tie one truth, the regenerating power of the Spirit, to the resulting truth; we will be enabled to do good works. The words *"so that"* are there to make the cause and affect clear and keep us from getting the roles reversed.

The *results* Paul is after are the good works we should produce. But what is the source of the ability to do those good works? Believing God! *"...so that those who have believed God..."* Believed God about what? About the *"regeneration and renewing of the Holy Spirit"*! The work of the Spirit is the cause and good works are the result. Titus was to confidently teach the people to put their faith in the Holy Spirit's work within them *so that* they would produce the good works that will result from His working within us.

**The result of the regenerating and renewing work
of the Holy Spirit is a new ability to do good works.**

Not What, But Whom

Look at Paul's statement to Titus again. Do you see the words
"whom He poured out"? Not *"what"*, but *"whom"*. All this
ability comes because He pours out the Holy Spirit upon us. Not a
truth, an idea or a principle, but a person, the Holy Spirit. The
Spirit of the resurrected Christ has been poured out on us that He
might live the life of Christ through us. Remember Rom. 8:11,
*"But if the Spirit of Him who raised Jesus from the dead dwells in
you..."* In Jesus are all the good works you and I desire to
produce. *And He is living in us by the Spirit!*

The principles of the New Testament are important because
they teach me what to ask, seek and knock for. But just knowing
them doesn't empower me to do them. This ability only comes
because God has richly poured out the person of His Spirit upon
us. Remember, as important as the Bible is to us, and it is
essential, the early believers didn't have the New Testament. They
had to trust the person of the Holy Spirit to live righteousness
through them.

This was the promise Jesus gave them around that table the
night before He was crucified. *"Apart from Me you can't do any of
these good works. But when I leave the Spirit will come and live in
you and He will empower you to do all we have talked about."*
The written word is absolutely important but it is the Holy Spirit
who makes living it possible. He is the Living Word!

127

Beware The Danger

Once again, the danger is to think the life-changing power of grace only refers to salvation. It is so common to see this as only relating to my eternal destiny. But Paul was clearly talking about how they would be empowered to conduct their daily lives.

We have been saved for eternity by grace, right? Yes, but grace is at work in us now producing the life of Christ. But it only works by faith. We must constantly be putting our faith, our expectation and our hope in this reality of *"Christ in us"*.

The *regenerating* and *renewing* work of the Spirit is something we must engage with on a daily basis. In our worship, prayer, meditation and normal thought life we must be aware of the Spirit who is alive and at work in us. The New Covenant is *"Christ in me"* by His Spirit, so we can clearly expect Him to be alive and at work in us, now!

Think of it. Every time you fall short, the Holy Spirit is available to renew your mind. Every time a weakness overpowers you, the Holy Spirit is ready to regenerate you. Every time you choose a selfish, carnal work instead of a "good work", the Holy Spirit wants to bring you near to God for washing, renewing and empowering. Learn to be a *"quicker confessor"* when you fail and draw near to God so you can be cleansed and empowered by the source.

Both To Desire And To Do

Remember our *"fear and trembling"* passage.

> *"So then, my beloved, just as you have always obeyed, not as in my presence only, but now much more in my absence, work out your salvation with fear and trembling; **for it is God who is at work in you, both to will and to work for His good pleasure."***
> (Phil 2:12-13 NAS)

128

Who is the worker?

"For it is God who is at work in you."

Who is doing the work in me?

God!

What work is He longing to do in us?

Give us both the desire and ability to do His good pleasure. Both *"the will and the work"*.

Listen to the New Living Translation.

> *"For God is working in you, giving you the desire to obey Him and the power to do what pleases Him."*

Both the desire and the power. Isn't this what every good *"Promise Makers"* Club member craves? The desire to say *"no"* to ungodliness and the power to say *"yes"* to godliness?

This work is only accomplished as we cooperate with the Holy Spirit. His job is to *renew* and *regenerate* us as we put our confidence and expectation in Him. His job is to change and transform us. God gets all the credit and we get the benefit!

I cannot put my faith in my ability and His ability at the same time. They are mutually exclusive. So I must put my faith in what I believe will actually work. I have learned by now that my ability runs out far too soon.

So He is the potter handling and shaping me. He is the worker working on me. And all this time I thought this was a *"Do-it-Yourself"* project.

Chapter Fifteen

The "Do-It-Yourself" Dilemma

On our journey into true grace, some truths about the process, about the *"how"* of becoming more like Him, are starting to fall into place.

Alright, fellow searchers, repeat after me –

"I am not the worker, I am the result of His work.

I am not the potter, I am the clay who is benefiting from His handling of me.

I am not the vine, I am the branch through whom His life flows.

I am not the source of the fruit, I am the conduit in whom His fruit grows.

I am not the river of life, I am a channel through whom His life moves.

And because all this is clearly true, I must not be the object of my faith.

Christ in me *must be the focus of all my hope, my confidence and expectation."*

Is This A *"Do-It-Yourself"* Project?

I confess I have been plagued by a "do-it-yourself" mentality most of my life. It has been such a constant companion with me, it seems entirely normal. I struggle to even think outside of that *"do-it-myself"* paradigm.

I did get some relief from this malady for the first few months after my conversion. I knew, beyond any doubt, that what happened *to* me and what was happening *within* me was the work of God. I knew I could not change myself. But I knew something was changing in me. And I knew the forgiveness and newness of life I felt within me was not a result of something I did but something that was being done *to* me.

I use the word *"felt"* here on purpose. In those early days I had no theological basis for what I was experiencing. I didn't know the Bible. I didn't know there was such a thing as "orthodox, systematic theology". I just knew I *"felt"* something had changed. Something *"felt"* fundamentally different within me. I could not define it any other way than to say I *"felt"* forgiven, I *"felt"* loved and I *"felt"* my weariness with life was largely gone, replaced by a peace and joy I had never known. I knew something was happening <u>in</u> me because something was being done *to* me. I couldn't define or explain it, but I certainly *"felt"* it.

The first Bible verse I remember memorizing, at the insistence of the family that had taken me on as their special project to love me into the Kingdom, was Gal. 6:9 – *"And let us not be weary in well-doing: for in due season we shall reap, if we faint not"*. (KJV)

I strongly recall that this verse was not a labor or a law for me. I felt like there was something new *in* me that was doing good *through* me. Loving people who were angry with me for my new beliefs, forgiving people who thought I was betraying them because I no longer wanted to participate in my former behaviors, giving my money when I had hardly any and reading my Bible even though most of it made little sense to me; these things seemed to come easily to me, they seemed to just be *"natural"*. Something was being done *to* me, *in* me and *through* me.

Without any Biblical understanding, I was somehow enabled to let Him be the worker and do a work in me. I couldn't explain it but I was enjoying the fruit of it.

Then I Grew Up...And This Became Hard

As a *"hippie"*, I was surrounded by people who held radical, reactionary views about God, church and morality. It was not popular to "convert" and begin believing traditional views about Jesus. And some of my friends' reactions were very strong, even hateful. Yet, it was easy to love those people and take their abuse because something within me enabled me to do it. Now I know it wasn't *"something"* in me but *"someone"* in me. It was the Spirit of the Risen Christ. But, of course, it came easily then. I was just a *"babe in Christ"*.

Then I began to hear teaching designed to help me *"grow up in Christ"*.

I was taught that we had to love others or God would not love us, we had to forgive others or God would not forgive us, we had to read our Bibles or God would not bless us, we had to pay our tithe or God would put a curse on us. And something within me began to change. What had formerly been easy to do, what had seemed natural, now became a chore, a job, a law, a *"work"*.

I Am Starting To Understand

I am beginning to understand what happened. In my mind, I became the worker instead of the workmanship. Instead of seeing myself as the clay, I began to think I was supposed to be the potter.

And I began to sincerely believe this was what God expected of me.

I know those who taught me were very sincere, and they were teaching out of their own well-intended desire to follow God. They were sincerely passing on what they had been taught. Their understanding of *"What God is really like"* and *"How He really feels about me"* was all they could give me. This kind of Christian life had been misrepresented to them; they believed it and passed it on to me. I certainly don't blame them. I sincerely passed it on to many, many others.

Looking back, I realize what I was taught fit into my natural view of life very well. Even though I was a *"hippie"* on the outside, I was an entrepreneur at heart. When I wanted something, I went after it until I got it.

As a child, I went from having multiple lemonade stands claiming it was for charity so people would buy more, to hiring other kids to run my newspaper routes so I didn't have to get up early, to stealing empty soda bottles from local gas stations at night and returning each morning with a red *Radio Flyer* wagon full to redeem them at 2 cents each at the same gas stations. I was a go-getter. All this before I turned thirteen.

By the mid-1960s, the cool thing was to be in a *"garage rock band"*. So I taught myself to play guitar and sing, put together a band and hit the club circuit. And I became quite popular in my little world because I worked hard and earned it.

"Earning by Works" Fit Well

The idea of working hard to get what I wanted fit very well with my personality. The belief that love had to be constantly earned fit in well with my upbringing.

At twelve years old, my two younger sisters and I were awakened one night and told that our parents were getting a divorce and we should choose who we wanted to live with. The following years saw my parents go through a total of seven marriages. They weren't bad people. They just didn't know any other way. Love had to be earned, it had to be worked for and, even then, it could be snatched away at any moment, for any infraction, real or imagined.

To believe that God demanded we earn His love, that we had to perform to His standards and only then would He reward us with blessing and protection, fit very well with my world view. *"Of course, this would be true"*, I reasoned, *"This is the way life works. The only difference now is I am working for God."* And though I began this Christian life with an amazing peace and joy at just being loved by God, I quickly learned this life was like any other. You worked hard to earn the good stuff or you just kept making more promises and working harder in the hope that one day you might get it right. Some days I did and some days I didn't and peace and joy was hit and miss. It seemed completely logical that the Christian life would be a *"do-it-yourself"* project. All the rest of life was.

Follow The Instruction Manual

It was as if God freely saved me but then He handed me a Bible and said,

"Learn to do all this! As you get good at doing this, I will bless you, protect you, love you and be near you. But only to the degree that you learn to do all this as I demand. I have saved you freely. But your life now depends on how well you learn to do all the right stuff in the right way.

135

This Bible is your instruction manual, your step-by-step guide on how to build your Christian life. To the degree you learn to do it and work hard to build it, to that degree I will be with you and bless you. I have given you all the directions. If you follow the directions and work hard, you will build a wonderful life that I will bless.

This is a 'do-it-yourself' project. I have given you the instructions but you must follow them and put forth the hard work to make it happen. I will be watching and as I see you doing well, I will bless you.

If you slack off or miss my 'perfect will', I am ready to punish you or, at the very least, I will withhold my love and blessing. And at the end of your life, I will set fire to all you have said and done and we will see how much of it burns up."

The frightening thing is I can find parts of Bible verses to defend all these ideas. I have done it for years. And yet, our Biblical heroes didn't seem to live with this nagging fear of failure.

In fact, they constantly taught against this type of life. They held out the real possibility of finding that *"easy and light"* life Jesus offered. They promised weary, worn-out people that God offered them a better life based on better promises for any who would believe.

Rather than a *"do-it-yourself"* life based on how hard you worked, the early church clearly believed in a *"Do-It-To-Me"* life. The life they lived depended on trusting and interacting with a God who loved them unconditionally. As they trusted Him and depended on Him, He kept doing something *to* them.

The "Do-It-_To_-Me" Life

The New Covenant offers the promise of a new way to live. If the *New Way* is indeed *"Christ living through us"*, then instead of a *"Do-It-Yourself"* project, this becomes a *"Do-It-_To_-Me"* life. Christ lives *in* you and He keeps doing something *to* you that results in progressive, continual change from within.

We have already seen that *God's Brilliant Plan* has been referred to throughout the Bible. The plan for God to come and live through human beings was not an afterthought. This *Brilliant Plan* was His idea from before the beginning.

The process of God doing something *to* people so He could love and fellowship them began in the Garden. He clothed Adam and Eve's nakedness to remove their sense of shame so He could again fellowship them. God did this *to* them. God promised Abraham He would do something *to* him and *through* him that would result in a righteous relationship and a promised son. Moses said God would do something *to* us that would change our hearts and enable us to love and obey Him (Deut. 30:6). Jeremiah said God would do something _to_ us that would change our hearts and enable us to be His people (Jer. 31:31). Ezekiel said God would do something _to_ us that would change us and make us different (Ezk. 11:19-20). Isaiah said God would do something _to_ us that would result in something so good that our own feeble human efforts would look like filthy rags in comparison (Is. 64:6). Each of these prophets spoke of what God wants to do _to_ us that will result in change: progressive and increasing change.

The whole purpose of Jeremiah's *"potter and clay"* experience was to demonstrate that the *New Way* is supposed to be about inviting the Potter to keep doing something *to* us. And what He does *to* us will progressively and increasingly change us as we keep interacting with Him.

137

Can you see it? Can your heart grab on to it?

This is the great adventure of living a *"Do-It-_To_-Me"* life.

Here's Your Helper

Sitting around the table that last night, Jesus clearly promised them that the Spirit would come into them and do things *to* them. Jesus didn't say *"I have the way, the truth and the life"*. He said *"I am the Way, the Truth and the Life"*. As He lives *in* us, the way, the truth and the life are doing something *to* us.

He told them something would happen *to* them that would result in an ability to produce fruit. More importantly, Jesus said their ability to obey Him would come directly from something that would be done *to* them by the Helper He was sending.

In John 14, sitting around the table on that last night, He said, *"If you love me, you will be enabled to obey me. And I will send you the Helper, who has been with you but He shall be in you."*

You will be enabled to obey me? How will we be enabled to do that?

"The Helper will come into you."
The Helper? What will He help us do? Obey!

"You will be able to obey me because I am
going to send you the One who can help you do it."

He will do something *to* us from the *inside* that will enable us to obey on the *outside*. He will keep changing us from the inside out. He will keep transforming us from the inside out. He will keep doing something *to* us that will keep making us different. It's the *New Way* of living and it will produce an *easy and light* life filled with *peace* and *joy*!

What A Brilliant Parent

This is *God's Brilliant Plan.*

He says, *"I want you to spend eternity with Me. But nothing can be with Me that is not like Me. So you must become like Me. But you cannot accomplish this. Your feeble human efforts cannot make you like Me. So I will come and live My nature and life through you. You will become like Me because I will make you like Me."*

This is brilliant. What a perfect plan. I wish I could have parented my children this way. I would have been a brilliant parent.

"Alright kids, Daddy wants you to become like him. I want you to be mature, wise and trustworthy. I want you to be able to make adult decisions, right now. But since you are not able to do that, I will put myself inside you and live my grownup life through you. I will put my ability in you."

What a brilliant plan for parenting. Of course, I could not do that as a parent but God can. And He does, for any who will believe in the *New Way*. This is the *Brilliant Plan* He prepared for us from before the beginning! And it is available to all who will take Him at His word and believe the New Covenant really is *"Christ in us, the hope of glory"*!

This is why Paul told us God did not pour out a truth, an idea or a concept. He poured out the Person of the Holy Spirit who *regenerates* and *renews* us. These are things the Spirit wants to keep doing *to* us.

Could this be, at least in part, what Paul meant when he talked about the *"simplicity of the Gospel"*? Could he have been talking about a process, a *Brilliant Plan*, where God does all this *to* us and our lives manifest the results?

If this is true, it would mean we are supposed to be *"receivers"* instead of *"producers"*; letting something be done *to* us instead of laboring to do something in our own power. This would mean that God has a plan to progressively change us, continually transform us and that He somehow wants to do all of this *to* us.

If this is true, then it seems I have been very wrong in thinking that the Christian life was some kind of a "do-it-yourself" project when it is, in fact, a *"do-it-to-me"* lifestyle. It appears my wisest response is to say, *"Here I am, Lord, please do something **to** me!"*

Although, it does make me wonder; just what is He going to do to me?

Chapter Sixteen

The "Do-It-To-Me" Solution

Throughout the Old Testament, God uses a variety of names to reveal His nature and character. He does this to communicate to His people *"What I am really like"* and *"How I really feel about you"*.

Each name begins with "Jehovah", "Yahweh", the "LORD". This is done so we will be very clear about just who it is we are dealing with. This is the *"Lord God"* who owes us nothing. This is the *"Lord God"* who is not under any obligation to any man. Yet, this is also the same *Lord God* who has made unbreakable promises to us out of His love for us.

And why does He love us? Just because He wants to. There is no other explanation for God's unconditional love except that He chooses to love us. He chose to set His love upon us because it's His nature to want a family to love (Deut. 7:7, Titus 3:4 and many others). This should be great news because if God's love depends on His nature then it does not depend on ours. And out of this inexplicably divine love, He chooses to *do things for us* that we cannot possibly do for ourselves.

This is why each of these names is important. They tell us something about what God wants to do *for* us...*when we cannot do it for ourselves.* God chose to introduce each of these names in times when Israel was in desperate need. Each of these names reveals something He wanted to do *for* them at the moment of their greatest need.

Although we can expect to experience partial fulfillment of these names in our lives now, we will not experience the fullness of each name until we burst into eternity and stand in the fullness of His presence. The *"down payment"* here is good, but the fulfillment there will be beyond comprehension.

The God Who *"Will"* When I Cannot

Notice each one of these names begins with *"Jehovah"* to remind us He doesn't *have* to do anything for us. Then it is followed by a description of the very thing He *wants* to do *for* us when we cannot do it *for* ourselves. He wants us to know that He is the God who will, when we cannot.

(The following is not intended to be a detailed study on the names of God. There are many variations in spelling and various shades of meaning, but I have tried to choose the most simple and commonly used definitions.)

Jehovah Jireh – The God who provides for you...*when you cannot provide for yourself.*

Jehovah Rapha – The God who heals you...*when you cannot heal yourself.*

Jehovah Shalom – The God who gives you peace...*when you cannot produce peace on your own.*

Jehovah Nissi – The God who wins the victory...*when you cannot win the battle by your best effort.*

Jehovah Shammah – The God who is present with you...*when you cannot earn His nearness by good behavior.*

Jehovah Sid kannu – The God who gives you right standing with Him...*when you cannot make yourself right enough for the Most Holy God.*

Each of these names tells us about something God will do *for* us *when we cannot do it for ourselves.* If we can do these things for ourselves then we don't need God to do them for us. These names are all about God's ability and *desire* to do *for* us what we cannot do *for* ourselves.

God's Desire To Do Things *For* Us

This has been a major revelation to me on my journey –

God really *likes* to do for me what I cannot possibly do for myself.

This belief does not come naturally to me. I constantly have to fight to wrap my brain around this idea. Because He is my *Father,* I don't have to convince Him to help me, coerce Him to help me or go on a hunger strike to get Him to help me. He really, really wants to help me. He *desires* to do these things *for* me.

Fervent prayer, joyful thanksgiving, and fasting are all important activities for me because they help refocus my life on how completely dependent I am upon Him for everything. Those activities help drive me to the One who wants to change me, but they don't change Him. And those things don't convince Him to help me. He helps me because He *wants* to help me. He actually *likes* to help me!

Jesus made this very clear by saying things like, *"Fear not, little flock, it is the Father's good pleasure to give you the kingdom"* (Luke 12:32). What an amazing concept. It gives God pleasure to provide for us, take care of us and do for us what we cannot possibly do for ourselves.

Pleasure? That is not a word many of us are comfortable with ascribing to the Holy God. Yet, Jesus uses it when describing how the Father feels about us. Jesus says it gives Him pleasure. Paul uses it repeatedly when describing how God feels about working His plan in us. He says God gets great pleasure out of working His purpose in our lives. John quotes the heavenly choir in Revelation as they declare that it gave God great pleasure just to create us. Can you imagine it? It gives God pleasure just that you exist?!

I have not always believed this. I have always *said* I believed this but I have not always actually believed this. For many years I secretly struggled with the idea that God loved me because He *had* to. He said He loved the whole world and I happened to be a part of the world so He *had* to love me. I have often fought with the idea that God *"loved"* me in some theological sense but He didn't really *"like"* me all that much.

But then the Holy Spirit takes me back to the night before Jesus was crucified and I hear Him praying, *"...so that the world may know that You sent Me, and loved them, even as You have loved Me."* Think of it, He wants us to know that the Father loves us just as He loves Jesus! Not a different love, not a lesser love, but He loves us just as He loves Jesus! And then, again, just moments later, He says, *"...so that the love with which You loved Me may be in them and I in them"* (John 17:23-26 NAS).

The same love, the same way! Amazing and hard to comprehend, which is why we need the Spirit to keep pouring it into our hearts and renewing our minds. As I discover that He wants me to truly enjoy this *easy* and *light* life of *Christ living in me,* I am also beginning to see something else He wants me to enjoy: the same love the Father has for Jesus, He has for me! That same love is *in* me! And because of God's great love for me, He not only wants to do things *for* me, *He wants to something to me.*

God's Desire To Do Something *To* Us

These *"Jehovah"* names tell us about specific things God wants to do *for* us. And there are times in our lives when we desperately need each of these things to be done *for* us. But there is one *"Jehovah"* name that tells of God's intention to do something *to* us. There is one name that gives us the promise of a miraculous transformation being done *to* us. This name is found in Lev. 20:7-8. It is *Jehovah M'kadesh.*

This name tells us about something amazing that God wants to do *to* us that will change the very nature of who we are and how we behave. And this name deals with the issue that has caused me more heartache, and given me more relief, than anything else in my walk with God. Coming to understand what the apostles understood about this name of God has given me more confidence about the divine possibilities in my life than any other single truth I have learned. It is the key to living in the *"Do-It-To-Me" Solution.*

145

Be Holy As He Is Holy? Are You Serious?

I want to be holy. I want to behave in holy ways. I want to live in the promise of *"Christ in me"*, to experience the fruit of the Spirit flowing through me and the nature of God being seen in me. And I confess that I used to feel very threatened by Peter's statement that I must *"be holy as He is holy"* (1 Peter 1:16*)*.

If this is a command we are expected to accomplish then it is a very scary thought. I do not know how to do that. How do human beings make themselves as holy as God is holy? Throughout this journey we have been seeing in Scripture just how impossible it is for human beings to do that. So what could Peter have meant?

In fact, *"Be holy as He is holy"* is NOT what Peter said. It is another often misquoted verse which I believed in error for years. And this mistaken idea has long terrified me because it seemed so impossible for me, or anyone, to make ourselves as holy as God is holy. And indeed, it is impossible by human effort, even the very best human effort.

What Did He Actually Say?

Peter's actual statement is, *"Because it is written, 'You shall be holy for I am Holy'"*. Look at it again. *"You shall become...because I am"*. Do you see the cause and affect here? The effect, or result, is that we will *"become holy"*. But what causes, or produces, this result is *"because I am holy"*. There is a huge clue here in our search for the *easy* and *light* life.

This is not a threat but a promise! This tells us the *"what"* (*You shall become holy*) but it also gives us the promise of the *"how"* (*Because I am holy*).

Is it possible that because the worker is holy, He makes His workmanship holy? Remember, we are His workmanship!

Is it possible that holiness is something that must be done *to* us before it can be seen *in* us and be revealed *through* us?

Hang on to this thought –

There is something about the holy nature of God
that can make everything around Him holy.

"You shall be holy for I am holy" is a direct quote from Lev. 20:7-8. This is the passage in Leviticus where we find the name, *Jehovah M'kadesh*. This is the name that gives us the promise that something can be done *to* us that will transform our very nature. This name, *Jehovah M'kadesh*, tells us that something can be produced *in* us as a result of something being done *to* us. By quoting from this passage way back in Leviticus, The Holy Spirit, speaking through Peter, made an important connection between this special name of God and our ability to become holy. This name for God is another important clue in our search.

Here's The Plan

Look at the whole passage of 1 Peter 1:10-16 in the New American Standard. Take note of how Peter connects the revelation of grace, *Christ living in us*, to how holiness will actually be produced in us. Remember, we already have a pretty good idea of *what* we are supposed to become. We are searching for the *"how to become"*.

The passage ends with the amazing promise that we will *"become holy"*. That is the result, or effect, we are after; holiness. But the process begins with what causes the effect –

"...the prophets who prophesied of the <u>grace</u> that would come to you made careful searches and inquiries, seeking to know what

147

person or time the Spirit of Christ within them was indicating as He predicted the sufferings of Christ and the glories to follow. It was revealed to them that they were not serving themselves, <u>but you</u>, in these things which now have been announced to you through those who preached the gospel to you by the Holy Spirit sent from heaven — things into which angels long to look."

Let's examine the *"cause and affect"* progression in this passage.

1)   The Old Testament prophets spoke of the grace that was to come.

     We have seen how Moses, Jeremiah, Ezekiel, Isaiah and many others foretold of this *Brilliant Plan* where God would come to live *in* and *through* people. This is *true grace*!

2)   The prophets could not understand how this *Brilliant Plan* would work.

     In their *Old Way* thinking they could not understand how this could be accomplished. External rules made sense to them. Almighty God living internally in human beings did not. As long as I keep looking to the *Old Way* of external rules and regulations I won't be able to understand it either.

3)   God spoke to them about the sufferings of Christ and the *"glories to follow"*.

We know Jesus' suffering was to take upon Himself the sins of the whole world. But Jesus told his men around the table that last night that following His suffering the Spirit would come and *live in them.* The *"glories to follow"* that the prophets spoke about point directly to bringing into action true grace; God's *Brilliant Plan* of Christ living *in* us and *through* us by His Spirit! True grace will produce the glory God is after; His life reflected back to Him from us!

4) Even the angels had a hard time understanding this *Brilliant Plan* of grace.

How could the Almighty God live *in* and *through* people? It even boggled the angels' minds.

With these words, Peter explains the *Brilliant Plan* God has been working for us and, more importantly, for Himself, since before the beginning. Then Peter tells us what we must do in response to the promise of this *Brilliant Plan* of grace.

> *"Therefore, prepare your minds for action, keep sober in spirit, fix your hope completely on the grace to be brought to you at the revelation of Jesus Christ."*

How can it be any clearer?

Fix your hope completely on grace!

Fix your hope completely on *"Christ in you"*!

This is what I must do. No one can do this for me. Even God can't do this for me. He has given every person the ability to believe (Rom. 12:3). But the choice to believe His Plan is up to me. He will draw near to me and empower me, but I must choose to *fix my hope completely* on His *Brilliant Plan* of Grace. I cannot choose my own method to attempt to accomplish what only He can accomplish in me. That is *Old Way* thinking and He will not allow it to work.

Of course, our adversary will do all in his power to keep us from *"fixing our hope completely on this grace in which we stand"*. So we find ourselves with a bit of a contradiction on our hands. If we are going to continue on this search for the *easy* and *light* life Jesus promised, we better get ready for a fight.

But, wait a minute; didn't Peter say *Jehovah M'kadesh* was going to do something *to* us?

Chapter Seventeen

Please Do Something To Me

I feel this plea rising up within me, *"Please do something to me"*. I feel a helplessness growing inside of me and I suspect God is very pleased with it. I strongly suspect this is His loving plan for me: to truly discover my utter helplessness, my utter inability to produce this *New Life*, my complete inability to live this *New Way*. Then, and only then, will I see that something serious must be done *to* me. It becomes my only hope.

Remember what Peter said – *"Fix your hope completely on the grace of God!"* There are certain things Peter says we are to *"add"* to our walk in God. Grace is not one of them. You don't *"add"* grace to the list of other things you believe. You must make true grace the foundation for everything else. You must *"fix your hope completely"* on it!

Grace, *"the unearned power of Christ's life being lived through me"*, is not a nice addition to my spiritual house, it is the very foundation upon which every other belief must be built. To do this in any other order is to miss the entire point of God's *Brilliant Plan*. To begin at any other starting point, no matter how true or well intended, is to guarantee frustration and disappointment.

And our adversary loves frustration and disappointment. God loves helplessness but our adversary loves hopelessness. And Peter understood hopelessness. After what he did the night Jesus was arrested, Peter understood what it meant to have your foundation ripped out from under you by something you have done that was so despicable that you would give up all hope. But Jesus never gave up hope in Peter's outcome. And as the Spirit came to live inside Peter on the day of Pentecost, a new understanding was born in this once hopeless disciple: the hope of God's *Brilliant Plan*, the true grace of God. So, with that firsthand experience, Peter declares, *"Fix your hope completely on the grace of God!"*

Get Ready For A Fight

Let's go back to Peter's statement of foundation, promise...and *warning*.

> *"As to this salvation, the prophets who prophesied of the grace that would come to you...predicted the sufferings of Christ and the glories to follow...therefore, prepare your minds for action, keep sober in spirit, fix your hope completely on the grace...but like the Holy One who called you, be holy yourselves also in all your behavior; because it is written, 'You shall be holy for I am holy'"* (1 Peter 1:10-16 NAS).

Now, look again at the promise, and *warning*, Peter gives them.

"Therefore, (because you are beginning to understand this *Brilliant Plan*) *prepare your minds for action, keep sober in spirit..."*

These are *"fighting words"*. These are words you speak to warriors just before the battle begins. *"Sober up! Focus your minds and prepare for what is coming!"* Peter gave this important advice because he knew once we choose to invest all our hope in this *Brilliant Plan* of true grace, our adversary will do everything he can to steal this revelation, and the transformation it will bring, from us.

I sometimes fear that many of my charismatic colleagues may be missing an important aspect of true spiritual warfare. I have a difficult time finding scriptural support in the New Testament for most of the Old Testament symbolism that seems so important to much of the current teaching about *"warfare"*. But I do see serious warnings throughout the Epistles about the battle that will go on in our minds and emotions if we choose to embrace true grace. We are warned to avoid the endless arguments about worldly wisdom or so-called logic and be ready for the constant accusing from our adversary in the form of fear, shame and condemnation.

The *"world"* will fight to convince us that *"this is too simple, too easy, it just can't work like this. There has to be more to it than this. You have to do something. Surely you have to do more than this. Just fix your hope on grace? It can't be that simple."*

These thoughts seem logical when I don't understand what grace actually is. This does seem too simple when I don't understand that grace is the Spirit of the Risen Christ alive *in* me doing a transforming work *to* me...that I could never do for myself! Something *is* being done, but I am not the one doing it. It is being done *to* me. Grace is doing something miraculous *to* me, *in* me and, more and more, *through* me.

If I am going to truly believe this *"word of grace"* then I better get ready for a battle. I better get serious about what I am choosing to believe because all of hell will fight to steal this from me. The last thing my adversary wants me to do is to experience a life of *true grace*!

The Bible says *"if the rulers of this world had understood this great mystery they would have never have crucified the Lord of Glory"* (1 Cor.2:8). This is not speaking about forgiveness through the crucifixion. God has always made a way for anyone to get His forgiveness. This is speaking of the *mystery of grace*, the wisdom of God's *Brilliant Plan* of Christ living *in* people. Remember Paul saying in Col. 1:27, *"...the mystery, which is, Christ in you, the hope of glory!"* This is what the powers of darkness feared most, that God would live *in* people. But the wisdom with which God implemented this *Brilliant Plan* was beyond anything they could understand.

What did Jesus say would result from His ascending back to the Father after His death and resurrection? *"The Spirit will come and live in you!"* The evil forces would have never cooperated in the crucifixion if they had figured out this *Brilliant Plan*. If they suspected their act would result in the Holy God coming to actually live inside of people they would never have willingly been involved.

**People living in true grace constitute a
most dangerous threat to the rulers of darkness!**

Grace Produces Holiness

Peter now makes the direct connection between the power of true grace and the holiness it will produce in us.

> *"As obedient children, do not be conformed to the former lusts which were yours in your ignorance, but like the Holy One who called you, be holy yourselves also in all your behavior; because it is written, 'You shall be holy for I am holy'."* (1 Peter 1:14-16 NAS).

How do I keep from being conformed to the lust of this world?

By fixing my hope completely on the grace of God at work within me.

How do I become holy in my behavior?

By fixing my hope completely on the grace of God at work within me.

Then Peter ends this amazing declaration about where our hope must be fixed and the fruit it will produce inside us by quoting directly from Lev. 20:7-8:

> *"You shall sanctify yourselves therefore and be holy, for I am the LORD your God. You shall keep My statutes and practice them; I am the LORD who sanctifies you."*

Please bear with me. I know we have been circling around this passage for a long time but there is a very important clue here. Can you see the connection between the *"what to be"* and the *"how to become"*?

"*You shall sanctify yourselves...I am the LORD who sanctifies you*".

It has taken me a long time and much agony to understand this amazing *"mother lode"* of truth; this vein of golden treasure that runs throughout the Bible. But it has truly changed my thinking and brought an *easy and light life* I never thought possible. Our Western minds are so very different than the Eastern minds of the

New Testament writers. We just don't think the way they did. So we have to kind of *"sneak up"* on the revelation about this name and nature of God. So, for right now, just hold tight to this thought – *"Sanctify yourselves...I sanctify you"*.

Just Knowing Is Not Enough

It is very important to understand that Peter and the other early apostles knew that just gaining more knowledge or mentally agreeing with a certain truth was not enough to transform people. And that is what must happen to us – ***transformation***.

Paul made it clear that just gaining more knowledge does not *transform* us; it *"puffs us up"* with arrogance. He told the Ephesians about a type of *"knowing God's love"* that was *"beyond knowledge"*. This *"knowing God"* is an on-going experience; a regular interaction with the Spirit living in us, giving us revelation and producing *transformation* in us.

When Peter urges us to *"fix our hope completely on grace"* he is talking about a dynamic life of interacting with the Spirit of Christ who is living in us. In this passage he actually brings us back to this strange name of God, *Jehovah M'kadesh*. Peter is writing about the result of *Jehovah M'kadesh* doing something *to* us that will *transform* us. This is the promise of this unique name for God.

But who is *Jehovah M'kadesh*? Again, I have to admit I don't understand things the way the early writers understood them. Obviously, Peter quoted Lev.20:7-8 because it meant something very important, both to him and to the Holy Spirit who inspired him to quote it. What could it be?

Who Is Jehovah M'kadesh?

Lev.20:7-8-*"You shall sanctify yourselves therefore and be holy, for I am the LORD your God. You shall keep My statutes and practice them; I am the LORD who sanctifies you."* (NAS)

The Hebrew words for *"sanctify"* and *"holy"* are almost identical. The only practical difference is *"sanctify"* is a verb and *"holy"* is a noun. *"Holy"* is what we are to *be* and *"sanctify"* is the activity of *becoming*. But how do we become more holy? How are we being sanctified?

This phrase, *"The Lord who sanctifies you"* is actually another name of God made from two Hebrew words, *Jehovah M'kadesh*. These two words literally mean, *"The God who makes men holy"*.

Wait. Don't read on yet. Think about those words a little more.

"I am the God who makes people holy".

David used the word *"Selah"* throughout the Psalms which literally means, *"Pause, wait a minute...think about that for a moment before proceeding"*.

"I am the God who makes people holy!" (Selah)

I believe the most practical understanding of this verse is –

*"You must become holy in order to be My people because I am the holy God. But I have good news. You will become holy and you will be enabled to keep my commandments because **I am the God who makes people holy!"***

"The God Who Makes People Holy"?!

Could this possibly be true? Could God possibly be saying that anyone who sticks with Him will become holy because He will *make* them holy? Absolutely! This is exactly what Peter said God was telling us in Lev. 20:7-8.

This is where it would be completely appropriate for us to yell out at the top of our lungs, *"Father, please do this to us!"* and know that the Almighty God's response is *"Good News, I am the God who does this to my people!"*

As a *"reverend"* I would say, *"Amen"*. But as an old hippie this is where I shout *"Far out!"*

Hope In A Most Unlikely Place

Think of it. In the middle of the *"book of the Law"*, Leviticus, we find the greatest hope for our weary, worn out souls. Right in the middle of the most demanding, depressing list of "dos and don'ts" you ever saw, there is this amazing promise. And it took the Holy Spirit a few thousand years later to uncover it as He pulls all the pieces of God's *Brilliant Plan* together and presents it to weary, worn out searchers. This really has been God's plan all along.

Remember, this is the part of the Old Testament that lists the regulations and requirements for nearly everything. There is a law in Leviticus for how to wash your hands, how to fix your food, how to pay a man who gets hurt while working on your house, even how to go to the bathroom while wandering in the wilderness! When you read through the first nineteen chapters of Leviticus, if you can get through them without falling asleep, you begin to think there is just no way you could ever do all these things correctly.

But then you get to 20:7-8 and you are given this most amazing promise! *"I am the God who makes people holy. I am the God who will do all this to you. I am the God who will do to you what you cannot do to yourself! I will live in you and make you holy like Me!"*

Of course, they couldn't really understand this back then. It was all there but it was hidden in shadow and type. The prophets didn't realize what they prophesying. Even the angels couldn't grasp what God was giving glimpses of.

But after Jesus ascended to the Father and the Spirit, the *"Teacher"*, came, all these things began to make sense. The *"Teacher"* began to give revelation to the early apostles and connect all the dots throughout the Old Testament. Men like Peter and Paul began to see God's *Brilliant Plan* throughout the Old Covenant and understood that the things that once looked like threats or orders were actually promises of great hope.

Listen to Lev. 20:7-8 again –

"I have good news. You will be able to sanctify yourself by drawing sanctification from me. You will be able to obey me because I will empower you to do it. You will become holy because I am the God who makes people holy. If you stick with me, I will transform you because I am the God who changes people. This is what I want to do to you."

Hear the Lord God of heaven and earth say, *"I make people holy. So if you stick with me you will progressively become holy, not because of your ability but because of Mine. Not because you are so good but because I am so good. Who you are will change because of who I am."*

**Remember, holiness must be done _to_ me
before it can be lived _in_ me and be revealed _through_ me.**

A Trip To A Good Doctor

Suppose you get sick. You do everything you can do but your condition does not improve. You finally go to the doctor. After a battery of tests, the doctor comes in and says, *"Here's what's wrong with you. There is nothing you can do in diet, supplements, rest or exercise that will cure this. But I have good news. You are going to get well. You are going to get well not by anything you can do but you are going to get well by sticking with me...because I am a good doctor. It will be the result of my ability, my education and my expertise, not by yours. Like I said, you are going to get well because I am a good doctor!"*

This is what Jehovah M'kadesh says to us:

"There is nothing you can do to fix your illness. But if you stick with Me you will get well because I am the Great Physician. There is nothing you can do on your own that will fix your unholiness problem. But I have good news. You will become holy if you stick with me because I am the God who makes people holy! It will not be because of your might or your power or your wisdom or your ability. It will be because I am a good God, I am a good 'holiness maker'!"

This Is The "Do-It-_To_-Me" Solution!

We are learning that the key to living the New Covenant is in understanding that God comes to live *in* us and...*He brings all that He is with Him.* He brings His nature, His character, His personality with Him. So Peter tells us that the real hope of becoming holy is found in experiencing God, *Jehovah M'kadesh,* living in and through us. The God who makes people holy wants to live in us and He wants to do holiness *to* us so that holiness will show up *in* us. The power to be sanctified is *in* Him, He is *in* us and He wants to keep doing sanctification *to* us.

Remember, this is the *New Way*. And in this *New Way*, God wants to keep doing something *to* us that will result in transforming us, sanctifying us and making us holy.

This the *New Way* where –

He is the potter and we are the clay,

He is the worker and we are His workmanship,

He is the vine and we are the branches,

He is the river and we are the channel,

He is the light and we are the prism,

He is the God who makes men holy and we are to reflect His holiness.

None of these Biblical descriptions of God's relationship with us indicate a "Do-It-Yourself" Project. In fact, all of these relationships describe the exact opposite. They all describe a *"Do-It-To-Me"* Solution for our weary lives.

This Doesn't Just Happen Automatically

But remember, the *New Way* doesn't just happen automatically. And it doesn't happen because we memorize certain verses and keep quoting them for reassurance. The *New Way* works because we let those verses drive us to encounter this *Jehovah M'kadesh*!

Encounters with God happen because we keep engaging with the Holy Spirit. We must keep *"drinking from the fountain"*, *"soaking in His presence"*, *"swimming in the river"*, *"meditating on His beauty"*, *"contemplating His character"*...whatever terminology fits well with your church culture. But what is certain is this: we must *"keep on being filled with the Spirit"* (Eph. 5:18). This is what causes transformation.

I want to believe this. I want to believe that somehow God will do something to me that will change me. And looking at all these verses it really does appear that this is what the early believers believed.

But I keep fighting with this nagging thought, *"There has to be more that I am supposed to do, right?"*

Chapter Eighteen

But Surely I Have To Do Something

I am guessing as you have read through this book you have had occasion to think –

"OK, I think I am getting it. This is all about what God does and I am the beneficiary. God is good and He does all this for me. I get it. But surely I have to <u>do something</u>. It can't be this simple. Just tell me what I have to do and let me get on with it."

I understand the frustration. I lived with it for years and I still battle it at times. I want to *do something* to make this happen. I want to do step *A* so result *B* will happen. This gives me some sense of control over when, where, and how things happen. Oh yeah, and I want it to happen right now! But that is *Old Way* thinking, and because He loves me, He will keep frustrating my attempts to make the *Old Way* work.

I have also learned the hard way that until we get the *"first thing"* first, everything else will be corrupted and devalued. Grace, *the unearned life of Christ living through me*, must become the *"first thing"* or it will just become another thing in the long list of things we say we believe, but that actually have little real effect in our lives. It will have no real transforming power in our lives because, until we put first things first, we will not truly *"get it"*. We will stay mired in *Old Way* thinking.

Remember where we began. If we don't define things the way God defines them we will never be able to believe what He believes. If we don't believe what He believes, we can never live the *easy and light life* He promised. And we will not be able to encounter Him in the place where transformation occurs.

Love And Draw Near

There are things you and I must do to access the true grace of God in our lives. These are things no one else can do for us, not even God. But He has already enabled us to do them. The simple New Testament answer to finding the *easy and light life* in Christ is to *"Love God"* and *"Draw Near to Him"*.

Simple? Yes.

Easy? Yes, if I do it God's way.

Automatic? Definitely not.

Jesus promised that if we truly *love God* and regularly *draw near to Him* we will find the *easy* and *light* life. For us to successfully and continually *"love God"* and *"draw near to Him"* requires (1) **faith**, (2) **humility** and (3) **regularly interacting with the Spirit**. But as we have learned, these three things must be defined as God defines them in His Word.

The remainder of this book will address what you and I must *do* to regularly access the grace of God. Again, these three activities are *faith, humility* and *interacting with the Spirit*. They are activities; they are actions we must do. These are the things the Holy Spirit longs to empower us to do. We will be examining the Biblical definitions of each of these three activities, seeing how they work together and then looking for practical ways to implement them in our lives. But we will be asking the Spirit to help us see them, not in the *Old Way* of the Law written on stone, but in the *New Way* of the Spirit living in us!

First Things First – "Faith Towards God"

So far on our journey together I have been trying to overwhelm you with an avalanche of scriptural truth to prove beyond a shadow of a doubt that God has a radically different plan than what many of us have sincerely believed in the past. I have made every effort to affect your belief about God's *Brilliant Plan* because *faith* in His way of doing this is the essential starting point.

If we begin at the wrong starting point then it doesn't matter how good the directions are, we will end up at the wrong place. We have to start at the correct starting point. And that correct starting point is *faith*; absolute conviction that this *New Way* of living begins and ends with confidence in the work God is doing *in* and *through* us.

> *"Therefore, having been justified by faith, we have peace with God through our Lord Jesus Christ, through whom also we have obtained our introduction by faith into this grace in which we stand..."* (Rom 5:1-2 NAS).

Our ability to *enter* and *stand* in grace comes from getting our *faith* clear and firm. Nothing is more important. There are others things we must do to grow in grace but Paul declares our *introduction into grace* is by faith in what God actually promises. Nothing is more important than getting our faith clear.

We are *"introduced into grace"* by faith in what God has promised to do. This is the foundation. *"For by grace you have been saved through faith."* The miracle of change is done *by* the power of grace, but I access its work in my life *through* faith; by believing this is indeed the *New Way* God wants to work in me.

We must live in *"the faith"*. Remember, *"the faith"* is not some general belief in Jesus but the specific belief that the easy and light life is experienced in direct proportion to my belief that He lives in me. I must be convinced that any good thing that comes out of me will be the result of His work through me.

Remember, the clay must not get the roles reversed; the branch must not get the roles reversed; the workmanship must not get the roles reversed! Reversing the roles makes faith in the *New Way* impossible.

Biblical Dyslexia

We have a genuine learning disability as part of the human condition. Our limited, human logic tends to twist things around. We get the roles reversed. We turn the cause into the effect. When God tries to teach us His ways, we turn it around so that *"the ways"* (or principles) become most important to us when *He* wants to be most important to us. When He wants us to express His love by doing something good in us, we mistakenly think we are supposed to do something good to convince Him to love us. This is understandable since we have an adversary who is constantly accusing us, getting us to reverse the roles in our minds and then convincing us we are seeing God's expectations clearly.

As a result, we are too often saved by the New Covenant but live our lives in the Old. Because we approach the Bible from an *Old Way* mentality we reinforce our position by misreading Bible verses. We have a learning disability some have defined as *"biblical dyslexia"*.

An admittedly simplistic explanation of dyslexia is when the brain rearranges letters, words or numbers so it becomes impossible to understand what one is reading or looking at. But when the person with the disability doesn't know they have it, they believe they are seeing things correctly. It makes perfect sense to them. Or it makes no sense at all, so they give up. That is, until someone enables them to understand their problem.

We have already seen how many times we have read a passage and thought it was an order or a threat when, in fact, it was a great promise. Remember back to the previous chapter. Does Peter command *"You better make yourself holy"* or does he promise *"You shall be made holy"*? Is holiness something we must do in order to please God or does God want to *do holiness to us* because it pleases Him for us to enjoy His holiness?

What about our *"fear and trembling"* verse (Phil 2:12)? Clearly that is a threat from a holy God, isn't it? No, it's a promise about how He wants to put everything in us that we need in order to please Him; both the desire and the ability to do His will.

But these wonderful promises don't work automatically. We must believe these things. Our faith in Him and His work in us must be absolutely firm. But for our faith to rest in Him we must see His Word clearly. So our adversary attempts to cleverly confuse us with *"biblical dyslexia"*.

Let me show you how this disability works. We are going to read a passage that is intended to give us tremendous promise.

> *"Grace and peace be multiplied to you in the knowledge of God and of Jesus our Lord; seeing that His divine power has granted to us everything pertaining to life and godliness, through the true knowledge of Him who called us by His own glory and excellence. For by these He has granted to us His precious and magnificent promises, so that by them you may become partakers of the divine nature, having escaped the corruption that is in the world by lust."* (2 Peter 1:2-5 NAS)

167

That is the way the passage is written. Yet, for years I assumed it meant this –

"If you will work hard to overcome the lust that is in the world then you can become a partaker of the divine nature. As you overcome your lust and earn the right to partake of the divine nature, then you can make the magnificent promises work for you. And that will eventually result in getting to know the true knowledge of God."

If I were sitting with you, talking to you right now, I would insert a *"pregnant pause"* right here...

I would wait, wait, wait...and hope that a light bulb would begin to shine over your head.

Do you see what I did with that passage? I turned it around. I reversed it. I took the benefits at the end and made them the requirements at the beginning. I took the intended results and turned them into the means to get the results. I took what God does and made it what I have to do. I took what He does first and turned it into what I have to do first. I took everything that was about Him and made it about me. I didn't mean to do that. I didn't know how wrong I was when I did that. I did that because I have a learning disability. And only the *"Teacher"*, the Spirit, can help me overcome it.

Let's read it again –

"Grace and peace be multiplied to you in the knowledge of God and of Jesus our Lord; seeing that His divine power <u>has granted</u> to us everything pertaining to life and godliness, through the true knowledge of Him who called us by His own glory and excellence. For by these He <u>has granted</u> to us His precious and magnificent promises, so that by them you <u>may become</u> partakers of the divine nature, having escaped the corruption that is in the world by lust." (2 Peter 1:2-5 NAS)

Look at it again in the correct order –

1) Grace and peace are multiplied (*increased)* to us as we grow in "knowing God"; learning *"What He is really like"* and *"How He really feels about us".*

2) He has *already* given us everything we need for life and godliness. It's all *in* us because He is *in* us and everything He is, is already *in* us. This is where Peter starts!

3) We are enabled to realize that He has *already* given us everything we need for life and godliness as we come to know the *"true knowledge"* of Him; *"What He is really like"* and *"How He feels about us".*

4) Because He has *already* done this *for* us and *in* us, we *already* have His magnificent promises so we can enjoy this *easy* and *light* life. We don't earn the promises or convince Him to give them to us, we *already* have them.

5) He expects us to simply *believe* these promises. That is what you do with promises, just believe them. As we believe them, we become *partakers of His divine nature.* This is the interaction we must be regularly doing with the Holy Spirit; *"partaking".* This is how we *"grow in grace".* We must regularly partake of the One who lives in us.

6) Our *focus* is to be on growing in our ability to *partake* of His divine nature, not in overcoming the corruption of this world. Christ's sacrifice has already paid the price for the corruption of this fallen world. We are to *"set our minds on the Spirit".* (Col. 2:3, Rom. 8:6-7)

Notice what He has already done for us –

He has already given us everything needed to produce life and godliness; and He has already given us His magnificent promises.

Now notice what we must progressively do –

We must grow in the true knowledge of Him and learn to partake more and more of His divine nature.

The natural result of believing what God has already done and then doing the part we must do is this: *we are enabled to overcome the lust that is in this world*!

And it is all the result of being rooted and grounded in *the faith* concerning what is already in us, *humbling* ourselves by putting our confidence in Him instead of ourselves and growing in our *interaction* with His Spirit who lives in us!

The Dyslexic Dilemma – Good Works Get In The Way

Biblical dyslexia causes us to reverse things, to twist them around. Every time I get it twisted around and start at the end of the equation instead of the beginning, I mess it up. And until someone shows me my learning disability, I just don't see that I have a problem. It looks completely logical to me and I will argue my position religiously.

I know it's hard to grasp. However, the very things God has guaranteed that true grace will produce in our lives *(good works)* can become the very things that blind us as to how true grace works. Every time I try to turn the *"results"* into the *"means"*, I mess things up and corrupt my ability to see clearly. Holiness is not the *means* of knowing God. Holiness is the *result* of knowing

God. I don't *earn* God's presence by my holiness. God's presence in my life *produces* holiness. The *cause* is partaking of the Spirit; the *result* is I become more and more like Him.

While holding a series of meetings in a small town in southern Illinois, we had several local pastors visit and listen to my teaching. Though the response was mostly wonderful, one pastor had serious problems with what I taught and left this message on the host pastor's telephone answering machine:

"I feel I need to warn you that you have a heretic speaking at your church. He is leading your people astray. What he doesn't understand is that you don't get good by getting God. You can only get to God by getting good."

Read that statement again – *"...you don't get good by getting God. You can only get to God by getting good."*

I don't know of any single sentence that sums up the *Old Way* thinking more succinctly than this; *"You can only get to God by getting good...first"*. If this were true, we would all be hopeless! And though few people would ever dare say this so clearly (and out loud!), many, if not most of God's kids live this way. *"If I can just try harder and get good enough, I know I will experience more of God in my life."*

This reversed thinking sums up the *dyslexic dilemma*. We turn things around so that the *means* becomes the *result*. This pastor truly believes the way a person gets more of God in their life is to make themselves good enough to deserve Him. And that makes perfect sense to him. But he didn't answer the age old question; *how good is good enough*? The *Old Way* of the Law says it must be perfect, 100%. We can't do that.

The wonderful truth of the *New Way* is that *"goodness"* is a fruit of the Spirit. Goodness is the *result* a believer experiences as they draw life from the Vine. The *result* of becoming *"good"* is produced by the *means*; which is –

1) **Faith** to believe He wants to produce goodness in me;
2) **Humility** to confess my inability to produce goodness; and
3) **Interacting** with the Spirit for His ability to transform me.

This sincere pastor just got the roles reversed. But that reversal is deadly. And you can find parts of Bible verses to support this view. But only disjointed parts, not the whole. The whole revelation of the Word tells us the Good News that *what is right about God will fix what is wrong with me; what is good about God will fix what is bad about me; what is holy about God will fix what is unholy about me!*

Good Works And Dead Works Look The Same

The drive within me to do good works *"so that"* God will love me, help me, protect me, or care for me, is the very drive that blinds me to the work of true grace. The New Testament writer of Hebrews understood this dilemma as the Holy Spirit inspired him to write about *"repentance from dead works and faith toward God"* (Heb. 6:2). Because of our *Old Way* thinking, we have assumed this verse actually means *"repentance from sin and trusting Jesus for forgiveness"*. That is not what the writer meant at all.

Dead works should be defined as the good things we do in order to prove to God we are worthy of His love or to convince Him we deserve His care. *Dead works* are good things done to earn His presence; good things done to make us worthy of His protection; good things done to convince Him we are really serious about obeying Him; and on and on and on. The dilemma is that good works and dead works usually look the same on the outside but the internal motivation is fatally wrong.

Paul spoke of this in 1 Cor. 13 when he listed several good things and then said that if he did them all, but out of the wrong motive, they would be of no profit to him. His good works are then *dead works*. He said if he gave away everything and yet was not motivated by the divine, *agape* love of God, his good works were rendered useless; *dead works*. The gifts would bless the recipient but they would be of no benefit *(they would be dead)* to the person giving them.

I have heard it said *"God loves a cheerful giver but He will receive from a grouch"*. However, the truth is He cannot bless or reward works done out of selfish or fearful motives because that will only further convince us that our wrong thinking is somehow right.

It's about here where I have, in confusing days gone by, spoken out of my frustration and said, *"Well, doing something good for the wrong motive is better than not trying at all"*. Of course, this assumes there are only two options – either keep doing good things for the wrong motive or just give up and be carnal. In fact, acting out of the wrong motive of fear does great damage because it further entrenches our thinking in the *Old Way*. But there is a third option; learning to live in the *New Way of the Spirit*.

How Can It Be Wrong When It Seems So Right?

Then I find myself asking, *"Why are good things done for the wrong motives, well... wrong?"*

173

Because they deny that God tells the truth! They actually judge Him to be a liar. They deny the truthfulness of God when He says He loves us with an everlasting love simply because He chose to and not because of any righteous deeds we can do. Righteous deeds are to be the *result* of cooperating with His Spirit working in us and we cooperate because of our assurance of His love for us. When our *"good works"* are done out of the wrong motives they say we don't believe God is telling the truth about why He loves us. Our actions deny that God loves us because of the goodness of His nature and declare that He loves us only if our nature is right and our deeds are good.

Good works done for the wrong motives also convince me that I can, by my effort, make myself like God. So who then is craving the credit? I am. By the way, this is the same delusion Lucifer fell prey to when he said, *"I will exalt myself and make myself like the Most High"*. And he enticed Eve into the same delusion when he said *"If you do this you will become like God"*. They mistakenly wanted the ability to become like God to be a result of their own ability.

So here's a question. Can it ever be wrong to want to be like God? Yes, it is, if I think I can achieve it by my own effort. It must be all Him because in Him we *"live and move and have our being"*.

Good deeds that are done *because* He loves me and is already living in me are righteous and pleasing to God. Good deeds done out of fear of rejection, because if I don't do them then He won't love me, or protect me, or care for me, etc., are *dead works*. This is the very reason Paul said, *"Whatsoever is not done in faith is sin"* (Rom. 14:23). Good things done for the wrong motive show my unbelief, both in His character and His ability.

174

The good works I do because I am driven by fear actually declare I don't believe He is able to produce righteousness in me. I am saying by my actions that I do not believe *"He who began a good work in me is able to complete it"*. These seemingly good things are not done in faith, but out of fearful unbelief.

The answer is not to stop doing good works but to get my motives straight with *"What God is really like"* and *"How He really feels about me"*! As I persuade my heart that the Word is true, good works are then produced as a result of my confidence that (1) He is alive in me, (2) He loves me unconditionally and (3) He will take care of my needs as I serve others.

The Old And New Ways Talk To Us

The *Old Way* says I must do the right things so He will love me. The *New Way* says because He completely loves me, He empowers me to do righteous things. The *Old Way* says I must do things that are pleasing to Him so He will be pleased with me. The *New Way* says, because I am in Christ, God is completely pleased with me and He is empowering me to do those things that He finds pleasing.

The *Old Way* says that when I fail to act righteously, then God is disappointed in me. He is angry with me so I must feel badly about myself and punish myself by sacrificing something I want so I can prove I am serious about repentance. The *New Way* says when I fail it's because I am trusting in myself and I need to quickly confess that misplaced trust, so He can wash me in His loving forgiveness and empower me to grow in true grace.

The *Old Way* always responds to human failure with fear, shame, and an expectation of punishment. The *Old Way* causes us to draw back from God and try to fix it ourselves to show we are worthy of His continuing love.

175

I Need A Good Brain Washing

The *New Way* causes us to respond by freely admitting our inability, throwing ourselves upon His mercy because *"mercy triumphs over judgment"* (James 2:13), and drawing near to Him to be washed by His Spirit and empowered by His life within us.

This *"New Way washing"* is what happens when we interact with the Holy Spirit and allow Him to cleanse our conscience from guilt, shame, fear and condemnation. *"...how much more will the blood of Christ, who through the eternal Spirit offered Himself without blemish to God, cleanse your conscience from dead works to serve the living God?"* (Heb 9:15 NAS)

"Conscience" in this passage can be more accurately understood as *"awareness"*. The above passage says we can have our *"awareness washed from the effects of dead works"*. One of the effects of dead works is to keep driving us to think that we must do things right so we can gain God's love and favor. The problem is we can never fully keep our end of that arrangement. So people are tormented with the question, *"If I have to do good for God to love and care for me, then how good is good enough?"* The accuser will make sure our best efforts never feel *"good enough"*. This is why we regularly need a good *"brain-washing"* by the regenerating and renewing of the Spirit.

This *"washing by the Spirit"* removes our self-awareness that says we must do something to fix ourselves before God will love and accept us. When we are no longer *"self-aware"* we become more *"God-aware"*. The more aware we are of the Spirit living in and through us, the more we see the fruit of the Spirit growing within us.

This *"washing by the Spirit"* keeps convincing me that God really wants to do *for* me, *in* me and *to* me everything I need done. Through this regular *"washing"*, the tormenting drive that I must do good works in the hope that He will love and accept me, is washed away. In its place comes an assurance that is rooted in the eternal acceptance Jesus purchased for me. Good works then flow out of my life because it is now natural. The natural thing is for a branch to bear the fruit of the vine it's abiding in.

That is what I want; a natural way to live the *easy* and *light* life. But I understand what Paul was talking about when he said he saw a battle within himself; a struggle between the Spirit and the flesh. I have that same struggle.

Maybe I need to get to that doctor we talked about earlier. Perhaps he has some medicine that might help me.

Chapter Nineteen

Take Your Medicine

If something miraculous isn't done *to* us, Christ's life can never be successfully lived *through* us. The promise of *Jehovah M'kadesh* is that He <u>will</u> do something *to* us that will change us and make us progressively holy. Paul's declaration, *"if a person is in Christ they become a new creation,"* rings with hope because it means something can be done *to* us that will make us different than what we have been in the past. The heart of what makes the Good News *"good"* is the hope that something can be done *to* us that will transform us.

True transformation is the hope of the Gospel.

With the hope that something can be done that will actually change us, we return to the upstairs rented room where Jesus and His men are talking just hours before He is betrayed. It was around this table that Jesus explained the most crucial elements of the *New Covenant*; this *New Way of the Spirit*, God's *Brilliant Plan*.

> *"If you love Me, you will keep My commandments. I will ask the Father, and He will give you another Helper, that He may be with you forever; that is the Spirit of truth, whom the world cannot*

receive, because it does not see Him or know Him, but you know Him because He abides with you and shall be <u>in</u> you" (John 14:15-17 NAS)

Let's look at some of the essential elements again –

"If you love me...the Father will send you a Helper...the Spirit...who will live inside you."

Here is the hope of the Gospel, the goal of God's *Brilliant Plan*. The Spirit will come to live in us, change us, enable us and transform us. But how does that happen? *A spirit living in me, trying to live through me?* That's a bit difficult to grasp. Just how is this going to take place?

Stick with me here. I am not attempting to develop a deep theological treatise, but I am trying to clarify a way to practically understand what *we are supposed to <u>do</u>* to access the grace of God within us. We have gotten pretty clear on what we are supposed to *believe; God's grace is living in us.* Now we need to get clear on what we are supposed to *do* for this to happen.

This Is, After All, A Mystery

The *Old Way* says there are specific steps that must be done in the right order at the right time under the right circumstances. Nothing mysterious here. It's all laid out, step by step, in a neat order. Everything in the right order, at the right time, under the right circumstances. The problem is it never really worked. It couldn't work because we could never keep up our end of the bargain. Not perfectly. And anything less than perfect obedience, perfect *god-likeness*, made us guilty of breaking the entire Law.

In fact, the *Old Way* was never meant to work. It was all type and shadow, the school-master and tutor leading us to a specific goal; giving up so *Christ could live in us.* The *Old Way* was made up of word-pictures to help us understand something that can't be explained in a nice, neat, well-ordered package.

But the *New Way* is not like the *Old*. The *New Way* is the substance. This is the real deal. This is what all the symbols and types pointed to. This is now *"God living in man"*. And this reality of *"God living in man"* is exactly what makes the *New Way* such a mystery. The mystery wasn't the *Old Way* of shadows and types, though it may seem mysterious when you read the Old Testament. The real mystery is the *New Way* of *"God living in people"*.

Paul repeatedly explained the *New Way* as the *"mystery of the ages"*.

To the Romans he said *"I want you to be well informed concerning this mystery"* and *"...my gospel, the revelation of the mystery which has been kept hidden for generations past"* (Rom. 11:25, 16:25). To the Ephesians he said, *"You understand my insight into this mystery"* and *"pray for the boldness to proclaim the mystery"* (Eph. 3:4, 6:19). And to the Colossians he said, *"The mystery, which is, <u>Christ in you</u>, the hope of glory!"* (Col. 1:27).

Paul declared that this great mystery was not just for the Jews, but that God had always intended to live within Gentiles who would believe. Part of this great *mystery* was to unite believing Jews and Gentiles, and out of us all, make *"one new man"* (Eph. 2:14-16). The word *"you"* in Col. 1:27 is the plural pronoun, as in *"all of you"*. Paul understood that this great mystery of Christ living in and through human beings will not be completely fulfilled until the whole community of Christ comes to the *"unity of the faith"* (remember the meaning of *"the faith"*) and we function corporately as His body on the Earth with Him living fully through us. The corporate aspect of *"Christ in you, the hope of glory"* is of deep importance but it's a subject for another book.

Paul said this idea of *"Christ in you"* was a very mysterious thing. He told his spiritual son, Timothy, that he had to be able to instruct people on the *"mystery of godliness"* (1 Tim. 3:16). Paul readily admitted that the process that caused human beings to become *"godly"*, that is, how people become more and more like God; this is truly a *mysterious process.* And rather than apologizing for this, he rejoiced in it because this made it a genuine work of God and not of man. This is not a humanly reasoned, strategically thought out, step-by-step idea that well disciplined, hard working people can accomplish. This is a mysterious, miraculous work that only God can do by His Spirit. God has always intended this transformation to be *"Not by human might, not by human power, but My Spirit"* (Zec. 4:6).

When Nicodemus came to Jesus by night, he seemed to be struggling to understand Him with that same kind of legalistic, systematic, *Old Way* thinking. *"We see the things you do and we hear the things you say and we know there is something of God here. We just don't understand because it doesn't fit into the system we have been taught to depend on"* (John 3).

Jesus answered Him with a very unsatisfying explanation. *"The wind blows where it wants and you cannot see the wind but you can see the effects of the wind."* This is not only a very non-reassuring answer to an analytical, systematic *Old Way* mind, but it comes out sounding mystical, almost spooky. Apparently, that was exactly what Jesus wanted. He came to introduce the *New Way of the Spirit*, the *Brilliant Plan* where the invisible God comes to live inside visible people. *The invisible God living inside visible people?* You don't get much more mystical and mysterious than that.

"Nicodemus, here's the way it's going to work. The wind of the Spirit is going to blow into you. You won't be able to see Him but

you will able to see the results of His work." Of course, Nicodemus responded with the now famous response of all good disciples, *"Huh?!"*

As good disciples, we take a leap of faith here from the *Old Way of the letter of the Law,* into the *New Way of the life of the Spirit.* Somehow our responsibility in this process involves learning how to cooperate and interact with this invisible Holy Spirit. A Spirit we can't see. But we do have Jesus' promise that we will be able to see the *results* of this invisible Spirit working in our lives.

Back To The Doctor

In the previous chapter we talked about *Jehovah M'kadesh* saying to us, *"You will become holy because I am the God who makes people holy".* We saw the tremendous hope in this promise because it depends on the quality of God's nature and His work; and not on our nature or our work. Our job is to stay with Him and let Him work within us. It clearly implies something is working inside of us that we can't see. But we will be able to see the results.

We then drew the analogy of going to a doctor who gave us good news by saying, *"You are going to get well because I am a good doctor".* We draw great hope from that because we know that our return to health doesn't depend on our medical ability but on his. And he is a *"good doctor".* Our job is to stay with him (or her) and allow their expertise to work within us. A doctor's expertise frequently comes in the form of a prescription. After diagnosing our problem, a medication is prescribed. This clearly implies that the right medicine will do something in us we can't see. When you look at the pills in the bottle you can't see the results they are supposed to produce. But the results can be seen in our bodies as the medicine does its work from the inside out.

So we return to the *Great Physician's* office in a rented upstairs banquet room.

"If you love me, you will keep my commandments...the Father will send the Helper... the Spirit...who will be in you."

The word Jesus used for *"commandment"* is literally translated by Strong's Greek Dictionary as *"an authoritative prescription"*. A prescription is something a doctor might issue for medication. Through a prescription the doctor is saying, *"If you want to get well then take your medicine."*

The prescription would include the name of the medication, the amount of the medication, and what the medication is intended to do. But it would also include the instructions for the patient; what the person is supposed to do in order for the medicine to do its work. Implicit in the prescription is an understanding that there are things only the medicine can do and there are things only the patient can do.

If the patient can do what the medicine can do then there is no need for the medication. But the point of the prescription is that the medicine can do what the patient *cannot* do. The responsibility of the patient is to *take* the prescribed medication at the right time and in the right amount.

The patient cannot do what the medicine can do, which is to produce the right changes within the body to affect a cure. But the medicine cannot do what the patient can do, which is to take in the medicine at the right time, in the right amount.

Keep Taking Your Medicine

I am not attempting to establish theological doctrine here but to layout a practical process of how we can cooperate with grace by learning to interact with the Spirit. In a very practical way John 14:15-17 says,

"If you love me then keep taking your medicine...which is the Spirit...

who will be sent to live in you and help you."

Can you see it? *"I am writing you 'an authoritative prescription' so keep taking your medicine, which is the Spirit, your Helper."*

"Keep taking your medicine?!" Yes!

What is the medicine? *"The Holy Spirit! He is sent to live in you, work in you and transform you into My image."*

That's what medicine is intended to do; work within you, change something and make you well.

Remember, the patient cannot do what the medicine can do. No one expects the patient to do what the medicine can do. No one holds the patient responsible for what only the medicine can do. The patient should never feel guilty or ashamed for not being able to do what the medicine can do.

But the patient is held responsible to do something – *take your medicine!* If the patient will do what he is supposed to do, then the medicine can do what it is supposed to do. The patient won't be able to see the medicine working inside their body but they will be able to see the results!

Here is another huge clue in our search for the *easy* and *light* life – *"Draw near to God and He will draw near to you!"* In this *"prescription"* of learning to interact with the Spirit we find what we are supposed to do...and what only God can do.

So I Am Sitting In The Doctor's Office...

As so often happens in my life, I had been on a dozen airplanes in the past two weeks breathing the same air with hundreds of other travelers. I had spoken to a half dozen audiences, prayed for and shaken hands with hundreds of participants. By the time I returned home I had contracted a respiratory infection that left me with a high fever and a wracking cough.

I prayed, had my family and spiritual family pray for me, and then I went to our family doctor. She didn't scold me, rebuke me or tell me how ashamed I should be for getting sick. She examined me to confirm the problem, wrote out a prescription and sent me home with these words, *"Sorry you are feeling badly, but follow the instructions on the label and you should be fine in a few days."* Certainly, not all illnesses can be dealt with this easily, but the principle of the *New Way* is hidden right here.

She didn't tell me I was responsible to make my immune system kick into gear, make my white blood cells unite and drive the infection out of my body. The medicine was responsible to do all that. But I did have a responsibility, a very important responsibility. And if I chose not to do it, there is the very real risk that I could have eventually died from that infection. My job? *I had to regularly take the medicine.* That was my responsibility. Mine, and mine alone.

All analogies break down when taken too far, but the point should be clear. Our hope is in the work of the Holy Spirit within us. He can do what we cannot do. He, alone, can do the transforming work that must be done. And no amount of well-intended human effort can do what He can do.

But there is something only we can do; keep drawing near to God, keep being filled with the Spirit, keep setting our minds on Him and keep *interacting* with His work within us. This is a life-long activity so we must not be consumed with condemnation when we fall short in the process.

No Condemnation In The Process

Paul seemed to fully understand this process. In Romans 7 he talks about the frustration of sometimes not doing the things he knew he should do and often times doing the very things he knew he should not do. In the anguish of this contradictory behavior, Paul says *"there is a war going on inside me and I sometimes do not understand myself"*.

But he goes right on in the next chapter and says that he did not live in condemnation over these failures. Remember, condemnation is the *"fearful expectation of judgment and punishment"*. Paul knew his job was to keep taking his medicine. He describes this process when he says, *"There is now no condemnation for those who are in Christ Jesus...the law of the Spirit of life in Christ Jesus has set you free...the mind set on the flesh (human effort) is death, but the mind set on the Spirit is life and peace"* (Rom 8:1-7).

Paul had just explained the battle he was fighting concerning his own behavior but, rather than feel he had to make excuses for his struggle, he takes full responsibility for it and sets his mind on the answer; the medicine for his *"illness"*. *"I am in Christ Jesus so I know my failures have been paid for. I set my mind on the law of the Spirit of life in Christ because I know that the mind set on the Spirit's work produces life and peace...in the midst of the battle!"* (Rom. 8:1-6) Paul could not see the Spirit but he was fully expecting to see the results of the Spirit's work.

No Illusions Of Perfection Here

These early believers had no illusions about the lack of *"Christ-likeness"* in their lives or about the life-long battle we all face in the process of *"becoming holy in our behavior"*. In Phil. 3:12-13, Paul talked openly about not having achieved perfection and made it clear it would not happen in this natural life. The goal, he said, was pressing on in the journey and running the race. James had no problem saying *"for we all stumble"* (James 3:2). John had no embarrassment in saying *"if we say we do not sin, then we lie"* (1 John 1:8). Peter made it clear we are to keep growing in grace because we won't arrive at it all here (2 Peter 3:18). They all understood that perfection, *full Christ-likeness*, would be achieved only when we see Him face to face and He makes us forever like Him (1 John 3:1-3, Rom. 8:29).

And yet, they learned to live without guilt, shame and condemnation. They didn't excuse their behavior when it fell short because they understood this was a process of life-long sanctification and that *"we have a High Priest who understands our weakness"* (Heb. 4:15). This perfect High Priest would certainly have the right to condemn us, but instead, *"He is continually interceding on our behalf"* (Rom. 8:34). Instead of excusing our behavior, He intercedes on our behalf. Instead of condemnation, He gives us His divine acceptance and help.

This is the same High Priest who told Peter, *"Before the rooster crows you will deny me three times...but I have prayed for you and you will turn around"* (Luke 22:34). In that same conversation this High Priest talked about the *"medicine of the Spirit"* and promised them, *"He shall be in you"* (John 14). One of the results of this *"Holy Spirit medicine"* is a healing from condemnation where we no longer live with a *"fearful expectation of judgment or punishment"* when we do fall short. We can be constantly convinced by the medicine of the Spirit that Christ's sacrifice paid for all sin, once and for all!

Many people have enjoyed hearing me teach about Paul's dilemma in Rom. 7 because it helps relieve their own condemnation to know that a man like Paul had to deal with the same things we deal with. But my grandchildren love to hear me preach about it because of the time I so enthusiastically declared to a large audience that Paul said *"I frequently don't do the things I should do and I frequently do do the things I should not do"*. Then, apparently suffering from temporary insanity, I loudly declared to an auditorium filled with people that Paul knew what it meant to feel like *"do-do"*. The grandkids thought that was *soooo* very funny.

Also included on my family's recording of *"Grandpa's Greatest Hits"* is the time I boldly proclaimed that when we fall short of the goal of Christ-like behavior our accuser loves to attack us with embarrassment by pointing out our *"falling shorts"*.

"Falling shorts"?! Now that's a great mental picture to paint in a church service where you are fervently urging people to have a life-changing encounter with God. Actually, my wife likes to replay that CD when friends come over for dinner. It's part of her calling to help me so I don't think more highly of myself than I ought to think. For some reason she suspects I might be tempted to do that.

Drink Your Medicine

Paul clearly understood our need to keep taking the *"medicine of the Spirit"* when he wrote *"Do not get drunk with wine...but keep on being filled with the Spirit..."* (Eph 5:18).

Regardless of what you may think of *"charismatic overindulgence"* in the mystical aspects of being filled with the

Spirit, we can't argue with the Holy Spirit's deliberate comparison between the many physical results of being drunk with alcohol and the positive effects of being filled with the Spirit. This is not intended to in any way minimize the horrible results of alcoholism, but we must acknowledge that the Spirit drew this comparison for a reason. The spectators on the day of Pentecost had good reason to assume those people were drunk; they acted drunk. I doubt very much they would have been looking at a well-ordered church service and drawn the conclusion that these people had been drinking too much, too early. The Scriptures speak often of the symbolic *"new wine"* and Paul continued this word-picture when he wrote *"we are all enabled to drink of one Spirit"* (1 Cor. 12:13).

Alcohol affects the human body from the inside out. The *in-filling* of the Spirit changes us from the inside out. Drunken people don't feel pain as they normally would. People filled with the Spirit don't get hurt by offenses but are quick to forgive. Drunken people frequently don't remember what happened while under the influence of alcohol. People filled with the Spirit let the love described in 1 Cor. 13 flow through them and they don't keep track of wrongs done to them. Drunken people often get happy for no visible reason and sometimes become amazingly generous, trying to give away their money, credit cards and car keys to other patrons in the bar. People filled with the Spirit frequently have an overwhelming joy for no visible reason and become amazingly generous, cheerfully giving to others in need while having an unwavering trust that God will provide for their own needs.

Hope Of Being Changed

There is something inescapably mystical and miraculous about the Biblical examples of people being filled with the Spirit. There can be no reasonable disagreement that weird and wonderful things happened every time people were described as being filled with the Holy Spirit. Nor can there be any greater hope than what Samuel said to young Saul in 1 Sam 10:6 – *"The Spirit of the LORD will come upon you mightily...and you will be changed into another man"*. Three verses later it says *"Then it happened when he turned his back to leave Samuel, God changed his heart; and all those signs came about on that day."*

"You will be changed into another man...then God changed his heart..." This is what all former *"Promise Makers"* Club members crave to experience: to be transformed by the power of the Spirit and never be the same again. All this happened because a human being *interacted with the Holy Spirit* and it changed him.

Remember our earlier statement, *"There is something about the holy nature of God that can make anything around Him holy"*. This encounter with the Spirit dramatically changed young Saul. His only real problem was that he didn't keep it up. He stopped interacting with the Holy Spirit and went after a different spirit.

Some may choose to argue about *"baptisms and initial evidences"* but one fact remains; the early believers had an on-going *interaction with the Spirit* that kept changing and empowering them. This *interaction with the Spirit* enabled them to love their enemies, cheerfully and sacrificially give away their possessions, and endure great hardship with unwavering peace and abounding joy. They lived the *easy* and *light* life as long as they continued to *interact with the Spirit*!

And it transformed their character to such a degree that other people began calling them *"Christians"* as in *"Christ-like"*. *"Christian"* was not a name the believers chose for themselves. They referred to themselves as *"believers"* or *"disciples"*. *"Christian"* was the label unbelievers put on them because their behavior was so much like the One they followed. Clearly, the results of continually drinking the *"medicine of the Spirit"* had a visible effect on God's people.

It must have been really great to be so much like Jesus that other people called you *"Christian"*. Yeah, that must have been really great. But when I go back to that upstairs room where Jesus explained the heart of this *New Way*, I remember Him telling His men that the only way to greatness was to become a foot-washer; that the only way *"up"* was *"down"* and to really become great you had to humble yourself and become a servant to everyone else. Somehow *humility* must play a very important part in finding this *easy* and *light* life.

And I have to be honest; discussions about *humility* make me very nervous.

Chapter Twenty

Stop Pretending

Our responsibilities in learning to live this life of grace are clear – *faith, humility and interacting with Spirit.* These are things we must do. These are things God will enable us to do if we will just draw near to Him. We don't do these things with our own power because we can't. He will enable us by His power but we must deliberately and regularly choose these three things. He has given to every person a measure of *faith* (Rom. 12:3), He tells us we must *humble* ourselves (James 4:10) and He commands us to keep being *filled* with the Spirit (Eph. 5:18).

I doubt you remember the last line of the first chapter in this book. I really don't expect you to, it was so long ago. In fact, I had to go back and look it up myself. But here it is, *"So, just what is wrong with me?"* Being able to ask this question of ourselves and then genuinely wanting God's answer is a critical step to being enabled to live in the true grace of God. The Bible calls this *"humility";* and true grace cannot be experienced without it. As long as I keep pretending I can produce this godly life, Christ can never produce it through me. But if I drop all pretence before God, knowing it is not real faith and it will never produce what I long for, what do I do instead?

Grace To The Humble

We have seen again and again that our introduction into true grace is by *faith*. Our introduction, *our access*, into this life of grace is based on what we believe about God's *Plan*. We must believe God's *Brilliant Plan* is to actually live His life through us. We must be rooted and grounded in the confidence that *"He who began this good work in us, He will complete it"*. We don't have to understand how He is going to complete it, in fact, we can't understand it. But we must keep assuring our hearts that He will...and He is!

We cannot put our faith in our own ability and put our faith in God's ability at the same time. These things are mutually exclusive. If I put my confidence in my ability, then God's ability cannot work in me. Either He wants *us* to produce something *for* Him (The *Old Way*) or *He* wants to do something *through* us (The *New Way*). It can't be both ways. It must be one or the other. And I have to keep choosing which I will believe and which I will submit myself to.

Of course, Jesus made it perfectly clear by saying, *"I am the vine, you are the branches and apart from me you can do nothing"*. He wants to produce something through me. And every time I say from my heart, *"Apart from you I can do nothing"*, I am acting in humility because I stop pretending I can do this on my own. That kind of humility activates the power of grace, *the life of the risen Christ*, in my life!

Proverbs 3:34, James 4:6 and 1 Peter 5:5 all tell us the same truth.

"God opposes the proud but gives His grace to the humble."

Based on our understanding of the correct definition of those words, what does this passage actually say?

"God has to frustrate the efforts of anyone who thinks they, by their own power, can become good enough to be like Him. But He pours out the unearned power of His resurrected life into anyone who acknowledges they cannot do this but trust that He will."

Grace, *the unearned power of Christ's life*, goes to the humble but it moves away from the proud. God has to frustrate the self-centered efforts of the proud, but He empowers the humble. The unearned power of Christ's life is given freely to those who *choose* to humble themselves. If humility is this important, then I better find out how God defines humility.

So How Does God Define Humility?

Humility has gotten a bad rap because our adversary knows how powerful and how healthy it is for the believer. The Bible is clear; we must humble ourselves to God and to each other. Humility is supposed to be a defining quality of the believer. But we have to define humility as God defines it.

Humility is not shown by saying, as I am being given the *Salesperson of the Year* award, *"Oh, I really don't deserve this award, it was just luck "*. Humility is not shown by saying, as people applaud after my special song at church, *"Oh no, it's not me, it's the Lord"*. Humility is not shown primarily in what we do when others are honoring us rightfully. It shows up in what we do when we fail.

Because I have been a musician for most of my life, written several songs and recorded a number of music CDs, I am frequently approached by songwriters asking if I will listen to their songs. I am saddened by how many people approach me and say, *"I have these songs I have written...well, I didn't write them, the*

*Lord wrote them...He just gave them to me...I mean, He didn't **give** them to me...they're not really mine, they're His, but...*" About this time, I reach out and take the songs, say *"I'd be glad to,"* and walk away. And I feel badly for them because they are just trying act the way they have been taught, either directly or by implication. This is painful, but it is not humility.

My grandfather was an Assembly of God pastor for forty-seven years. In one church he planted, he had a dear saint who would come up at least once a month and want to sing a special song for the congregation. This being a small, country church with good ole country folks, and not wanting to offend her, my grandfather would allow her to sing. She always began by saying, *"Now, I know I can't sing 'cause I don't have no good singing voice. So I don't want y'all to listen to my voice but I want you to hear the words of this wonderful old hymn."* She would then bellow and howl her way through some song out of the *"Melodies of Praise"* hymnal and everyone would just *"suffer for Jesus' sake"*. Finally, one Sunday morning, after she had gone through her preamble again and said *"...I just want you to hear the words"*, my grandfather stood up and said, *"Then, please Sister, bless us all and don't sing. Just read the song to us!"* Apparently, she was right about not having a good singing voice. But she was not being humble.

How Low Can You Go?

The basic Greek word used for humility means to *"make low"*. It is the deliberate act of taking the lower place, not out of low self-esteem but because you esteem others as higher than yourself. Humility is a deliberate act only I can do for myself. Someone else can humiliate me but no one can make me humble. Humility is an action I must deliberately choose to do. And the act of humbling myself is both healthy and powerful because of what it allows God to do in response.

Humility is healthy because it allows God, the Heavenly Doctor, to keep correcting and adjusting me; it allows the medicine to keep working within me. Humility is powerful because through it I am denying my ability and that allows God to release His life within me. Only when I lay my life down can His life rise up in me. Only when I lay my ability down can His ability rise up in me. I must get low so He can rise up in me. John the Baptist said, *"He must increase and I must decrease."* John may have struggled with some questions near the end of his life but with those words he clearly demonstrated that he understood the basic process of true grace.

Humility before God and *faith towards God* go hand in hand. Phil. 2:5-9 tells us we must see this the same way Jesus saw it. He humbled Himself by taking the blame of the whole world. But He did it in faith that the Father would justify Him and raise Him up. The Father's response was to bring Him back from the dead, highly exalt Him and extend redemption to the whole world. If the Father justified and exalted Jesus for taking the blame for things He didn't do, how much more will the Father justify us for humbling ourselves and taking the blame we fully deserve? We must humble ourselves and take full responsibility for our failures, but we must do it in faith that God will forgive, cleanse, regenerate and renew us according to His promise. So then the real question is not *"are we to blame?"* but, knowing what the Father will do in us if we humble ourselves, *"how low can we go"?*

Jesus frequently talked to the Pharisees about humility and pride. The Pharisees knew a thing or two about pride although they didn't really *know they knew*. Jesus explained humility as the act of deliberately taking the lowest seat at a wedding and trusting that if the master of the feast thought you were worthy, he would move you up. Do you see how humility and faith must work together here? To do the act of humbling yourself you had to believe someone greater would raise you up. But the decision of when and where you would be raised up was in the hands of someone greater. And you had to trust that *"someone greater"*.

This is the humility the Word talks about when it tells us to *"Humble yourselves in the presence of the Lord, and He will exalt you"* (James 4:10 NAS). But He goes on to warn the Pharisees that if they *pretend* to be more important than they are, the master of the feast will come and demote them in the seating arrangement...in front of everyone! This example tells us something very important about humility; it involves learning to be *"un-pretentious"*.

Stop Pretending You Can Do It

It has helped me immensely to see that Biblical humility comes when I choose to be *"un-pretentious"*. The New Living Translation really helps us understand humility by translating James 4:10 like this:

"When you bow down before the Lord and admit your dependence on Him, He will lift you up and give you honor."

Admit my dependence on Him?! That is true humility; bow down and admit it!

This sounds just like Jesus saying to the guys around the table that last night, *"Apart from me you can do nothing. Just go ahead and admit it, boys. This is a medicine that will do you good."* There can be no pretending here.

He promised them they would bear much fruit, but not because they pretended they had the ability to be *prolific fruit-producers*. They would bear fruit only to the degree they stopped pretending, admitted their complete dependence on Him and trusted He was telling them the truth about how the Spirit would bear fruit through them. This was their only hope: stop pretending about their ability and believe that He would live *in* and *through* them. Pretending they could do it would only get in the way and drive them back to the *Old Way*.

So, because He loves us and doesn't want us to remain caught in the trap of self-sufficient pride, He opposes us when we act in pride but gives us His unearned power when we act in humility. So how do I know which group I am in?

What Do The Proud Say?

"Give me one more chance and I promise You, I will get it right the next time. I know that was wrong but I had a bad childhood. Next time I will try harder and I will overcome the bad influence of my parents, I promise. My wife just pushed me too far but next time I will ignore her and I will get it right. The pressure of the bills; and my boss doesn't understand how I work best; and if that criticism would have been constructive I wouldn't have reacted that way. But give me one more chance and I will act just like You because I am really serious this time."

Hopefully, since we have come this far in our search together, it's a lot easier now to detect the pride that is wrapped up in this way of thinking. *"Promise Maker"* Club members may be sincere but we are all just pumping up our pride. Listen to it again.

"God, give me one more chance and I will make myself just like You".

I have said this hundreds, no, thousands of times, and never knew the pride that was really motivating me. *"Stand back, God, and just watch what I can produce if given enough time."* I never meant it to sound like that and I never realized how much pride it took for me to think like that. But then I ask myself, *"How must this sound to the God who wants to freely live His divine life through me; to the God who knows I cannot possibly do what I am foolishly promising; to the God who wants to freely do all this through me?"*

Can a human being make themselves like God, no matter hard they try or how much time you give them? Of course, not! But my pride wants me to believe it's somehow possible. My pride tells me that if I will pretend long enough, somehow I will gain the ability. And the devil wants to keep me convinced that this is what God expects me to believe and confess.

This is what makes me nervous about some of our *"re-dedication"* services and *"re-commitment"* altar calls. It encourages people to crank up their will power, pretend they are capable of something they are not, stir up their misguided pride and make more promises they can't keep. And it reinforces the belief that this kind of self-effort is what God is looking for.

We don't do this on purpose. We don't realize this actually encourages pride. We've been deceived into believing this is the right way to think and act. We have followed the human logic that says this is what God wants us to do.

But, in fact, God must oppose this kind of prideful effort. If it would ever really work, it would destroy us. Our independent success would fully convince us that we can live apart from Him. Even limited success can keep us from seeing how utterly dependent we are on Him living through us; at least, as long as we can ignore that nagging lack of peace and joy.

So God, in His great love for us, opposes our efforts.

Imagine the young child trying to run onto the football field and play with the fully outfitted adults. To his young mind it looks like great fun and he believes he is truly ready to participate. To the mind of the father, it looks like broken bones and an emergency room visit. So the father hangs on to the back of the child's pants while the little legs churn and arms flail; and he finally runs out of steam. God must run us out of our own strength so we will bow low before Him and beg for His strength to flow through us.

What Would The Humble Say?

"Apart from you I can do nothing. I freely confess my sin because it shows I am acting apart from You. Thank you for already paying for it on the cross. When I act apart from Your life and power in me, I fall miserably short of the goal. Of course I do. I repent of acting on my own and put my faith back in You."

The humble don't pretend. They agree with the truth when it speaks against their cherished view of themselves. The humble quickly confess the inevitable failure of their own ability. The humble quickly confess what they know to be true: each time we act in our own strength we will fail. One of the goals of the humble who are growing in God's grace is to become *"quicker confessors"*. This is the heart of biblical humility.

I confess to you that I wanted so much to use the pronouns *"us"*, *"we"* and *"ourselves"* in that last paragraph. But I am just not there yet. You may be; I am not. But I am *"becoming"*.

Instead of promising God we will do better next time, we are much better off to stop pretending and admit the truth. *"Unless you change me, it won't get any better than this. That was me at my best, just filthy rags. This is not an excuse; this is me admitting*

201

the truth. Apart from you I can do nothing. And I am willing to reap whatever I need to reap from the bad seed I have sown with that kind of behavior if it will help me choose humility. I believe You live in me and I draw near to You, right now, for the transforming power of Your Spirit, which is my only hope."

Humility is the ability to stop pretending and admit the truth about myself without self-defense or justification. The humble can readily admit the truth about themselves because they trust their loving Father to justify them. This is what confession is all about; admitting the truth without self-defense and trusting in the forgiving, cleansing work of the Spirit.

The danger of self-defense is that it blinds me to the truth about myself and cuts me off from the transforming work of the Spirit. If I defend myself, my Father cannot defend me. If I justify myself, my Father cannot justify me. If I excuse myself, my Father cannot cleanse me. If I stubbornly cling to the belief that I can change myself, my Father cannot change me.

But getting mad at myself will just make things worse.

Chapter Twenty-One

I Am So
Mad At Myself!

"...for the anger of man does not achieve the righteousness of God." (James 1:20-21 NAS)

Here is another one of the many verses I misunderstood for years. Of course, when a person loses their temper and strikes out at other people, it's bad and not righteous. But that is not what this verse is talking about at all. This verse is speaking about the futility of getting angry at yourself when you fail and striking out...at yourself.

The verses leading up to this statement about the futility of anger speak about being tried and tested, how temptation turns into sin and the inevitable result of unchecked sin in a person's life. Then James tells us that the way to overcome this downward slide into sin is to be *"quick to hear, slow to speak and slow to anger...because the anger of man does not achieve the righteousness of God"*. James is talking about the anger we feel at ourselves when we fail in temptation and trial.

Again, we find this faulty thinking seems so logical. It seems right to say:

"I am so angry at myself for acting that way. And, Lord, I want you to know my anger shows just how serious I really am this time. See how mad I am at myself. I know how shameful it was to act like that. I know better than that. I don't deserve anything from You. In fact, until I fix this, I can understand why You don't want me near You."

Following this logic, I have told people in counseling sessions, *"Until you really get angry at your sin, you are not going to be serious enough to get free. God can't help you until you are really serious and you show how serious you are by how angry you get at yourself"*. As logical as this seems, this thinking does not lead me to the solution because it keeps the focus on me and my ability; or more accurately, my lack of ability to overcome sin in my own strength. The truth is, I show how serious I am about my sin when I humble myself by taking full responsibility for it and drawing near to God in faith.

Doesn't It Help To Get Angry?

Follow the faulty human logic.

I am mad at myself because I didn't behave like God would have behaved in the same situation. I am ashamed of myself for not behaving like a godly person should behave. Surely, the holy God is angry with me. Surely, a perfect God is ashamed of me. He is, after all, holy and I clearly am not. And, surely, the holy God doesn't want such an unholy person as me near Him until I fix this. And I do remember all those fiery sermons where I was told *"God is a holy God and nothing unholy can stand in His presence"*. So I crank up my will power and my promise-making ability, thinking this will fix my problem.

But, of course, it doesn't fix my sin problem. Not permanently, because true self-control is a fruit of the Spirit (Gal. 5:22) and I have drawn back from the Spirit by focusing my anger on myself. I can only have true fruit show up in my life as I draw from the life of the Spirit and let His life flow through me. *"Godly sorrow"* leads us to draw near to God for His help. But anger focuses on me and my wounded pride.

What my anger does do is further convince me that God is angry with me and waiting for me to finally get my act together and then He will draw near to me again. My anger also feeds my pride because it says once I get mad enough, this self-generated anger will give me the power to become like God. So I convince myself the power comes from me. I am just not mad at myself enough yet.

Faulty Logic

Of course, the logic that *"God is a holy God and nothing unholy can stand in His presence"* would then tell us that no one other than Jesus could ever experience the presence of God. And yet, the Bible is filled with stories of unholy people who encountered God in various degrees of His *"Presence"*. In fact, *everyone* who has ever encountered God, other than Jesus, was unholy. Some were far more *"unholy"* than you.

In the eternal sense, all children of God will be permanently *made* holy when we are completely glorified in body and soul at the end of this age and we will be made forever like the image of the Son. But in this life, the Holy Spirit lives in unholy people. Thank God that He does! We are being made holy by the very Holy Spirit who literally lives within us. The humanistic logic that God can't be near unholy people is wonderfully wrong! Our only hope of holiness is that *Jehovah M'kadesh* will keep drawing near to us and keep filling us with Himself.

Isaiah 6:1 tells of the prophet's experience in the presence of God and the realization that his lips were unclean and he was *"unholy"*. He saw this about himself because he was in God's holy presence. God's response was not to kick Isaiah out of His presence but to send an angel to cleanse him. Isaiah's responsibility was not to cleanse himself but to confess his uncleanness and...*stay in the presence of God for the cleansing only He could do!* That is our only hope: that the holy God will keep cleansing us as we draw near to Him.

Sin does not *"hurt"* God. It does not surprise Him when it shows up in us. He knows all things, all the time. The potter knew there was *gunk* in the clay when he dug it up. God says He is the potter so He knows what's still in us as His clay. Sin is not a *"problem"* for God because He dealt with it once and for all on the cross.

But sin is serious because of the damage it does to us; to our hearts and minds and to those around us. A human father knows the danger and damage disobedience does to a child. Our heavenly Father knows far better. The scripture is clear that when I refuse to acknowledge and confess my sin, my heart begins to grow hard and my conscience is eventually seared (1 Tim. 4:2, Heb. 3:13).

I must be serious about overcoming sin but getting angry at myself doesn't help. It's completely counterproductive. To truly overcome sin I should be serious about humbling myself and getting to the *Doctor* as quickly as I can.

Back To The Doctor

Suppose you called the doctor's office and the conversation went something like this:

"I would like to make an appointment to see the doctor."

"Certainly, and what is wrong with you?"

"Well, nothing...now".

"What do you mean, 'now'?"

"Oh, last week I was sick as a dog. But I'm good now".

"But why didn't you come in last week while you were sick?"

"Oh, I was so angry at myself for getting sick and I was much too ashamed at myself for the doctor to see me in that condition! But I'm good now, so can I make an appointment to show the doctor how well I am doing?"

We would all think that was a bit bizarre. But how often do we do that with God? We draw back when we mess up because we feel ashamed of ourselves and we are certain God must be ashamed of us. Knowing God must be ashamed of us, our shame makes us angry with ourselves. We think being really mad at ourselves will help us overcome the next time. Then God will stop being ashamed of us and He will want us near Him again.

But what we actually need to do is to stop pretending we can fix ourselves, get to the doctor as fast as we can and let Him do what He does best; *regenerate and renew us!* The Great Physician really wants us to come to Him in our weakness so He can forgive and cleanse us! But if we believe the Doctor will be ashamed of us, we won't go to Him until we can make ourselves *"well"*.

Blame Without Shame

Our adversary understands the power of humility far better than we do. It was pride that caused his fall and exclusion from heaven. But his pride took the form of the deceptive belief that if he tried hard enough he could make himself like God. *"I will make myself like the Most High"* (Is. 14). This was the same attack he made in the Garden, *"If you will do this you will make yourself like God!"* God had already created them in His image and given them everything they needed to live life and fulfill His purpose. If they lacked anything He surely would have been willing to give it to them. But they fell to the misguided belief that they had to do something in their own power to partake of the divine nature. It seemed perfectly logical to them.

Wait a minute; that sounds just like 2 Peter 1:3 *"...seeing that His divine power has granted to us everything pertaining to life and godliness"*. God joyfully provided all they needed for life and godliness in the garden. Anything they lacked, He would have added. They failed by acting apart from Him. Does that sound familiar? *"Apart from Me you can do nothing."* Paul understood this wonderful life of dependence on a Father who fully loves us when he said *"He who did not spare His own Son, but delivered Him over for us all, how will He not also with Him freely give us all things?"* (Rom 8:32 NAS)

Peter understood the amazing truth that God had already put within us *"everything pertaining to life and godliness"*. Peter also knew a lot about acting in his own strength and the shame of failing miserably. The night before Jesus was crucified Peter did what all good Christians would think was the right thing to do. When Jesus said *"You will all fall away from me"*, Peter declared his commitment, *"I promise I will never betray You"*. Of course, Jesus knew Peter was speaking out of his human strength; reasonable, logical, but just human ability. Jesus knew for Peter to find the strength of God, his human strength had to fail. And it did fail that night, miserably.

Years later, Peter tells us what he learned; God has already put in us all we need and if we will believe these great promises about true grace then we become *partakers of the divine nature!* *"...He has granted to us His precious and magnificent promises, so that by them you may become partakers of the divine nature"* (2 Peter 1:4 NAS).

Because our adversary understands that the source of true godliness comes from our willingness to be humble, *unpretentious*, before God, his second plan of attack is to convince us to be so ashamed of ourselves we draw back from God. We do that in the pretense that if we try harder we can do better. If you feel ashamed before God, you may confess, but you will have no faith to believe His promise that *"He gives His grace to the humble".*

Both Judas and Peter betrayed Jesus. Judas was overtaken with shame and killed himself. Peter took the blame and was enabled to write years later, *"This is the true grace of God. Stand firm in it!"* (1 Peter 5:12).

God has made a way for us to take the blame for our weakness, failure and sin without being destroyed by the shame, if we will believe Him. His plan was to put upon Jesus, not only the *sins* of the whole world, but the *shame* of those sins upon Him, also. Jesus willingly humbled Himself to the shame of the cross, hung naked before the world, taking the curse for the world's arrogant rebellion. Isaiah 53 says that in His death He was despised by all, rejected by all and that it pleased the Father to crush Him, laying the shame of us all upon Him. Why? So that when He died, our shame before God would also die, once and for all. As a result, we can come boldly before Him knowing we have a High Priest who understands our weaknesses and intercedes for us constantly! (Heb 4:15, Rom. 8:34) *We can take the blame without being crushed by the shame!*

How Can He Not Be Ashamed Of Us?

While we are in the process of *"becoming"*, in the process of being sanctified, He is not ashamed of us.

209

> *"For both He who sanctifies and those who are being sanctified are all from one Father; for which reason He is not ashamed to call them brethren."* (Heb 2:11-12 NAS)

This is us! We are the ones who are *"being sanctified"*. We are not yet done and we won't be done until we stand before Him and He makes us forever like Him. But because we are all of the same Father and He knows what we will finally become, He is not ashamed of us now. Jesus is not ashamed to call us, who are struggling in this process of becoming sanctified, *His brothers*! He is not ashamed of us now because He already sees us finished. *He sees us done!*

Time and space are creations for *"this age"* and they will both be done away with when God is finished with this age. Time will be *"rolled up like an old garment"* and there will be no need of a sun and moon to mark the passage of time. We will be made like God. God lives above and beyond time. One simple way to explain it is that God looks down upon time. The past, present and future are all available to Him at the same time. He is the eternal God, eternally timeless.

The Bible is filled with evidence of this truth and we need to just accept it. But if I think about it too much smoke starts coming out of my ears. I can't wrap my little brain around it. It is a cosmic concept beyond our true comprehension. However, one day we will see it fully. One day we will *"know as we are known"*. By the way, when you get to heaven you will not have a list of things you want to ask Him to explain. You will then know all things the way God knows all things about you now. *"...but then I will know fully just as I also have been fully known"* (1 Cor 13:12 *NAS*).

He Sees Us Done

Because God exists apart from time and space, He sees His purpose in us completed; even as He is fully aware of it unfolding in us right now. So here is more tremendously Good News; God sees us done, finished, completed in Christ!

> *"For those whom He foreknew, He also predestined to become conformed to the image of His Son".* (Rom 8:29 NAS)

There are two very important words in this passage; *foreknew* and *predestined*. The first means God knows what is going to happen because He is already in the future. The other means God demands that it happen because it is His absolute will. Because God *knew beforehand* what your response to His Son would be, He has *ordained* that you will be completely and forever *made* into the image of His Son! This is your predestined end in God. He already sees you done, finished, completed into Christ's image. And that will be our state of being forever! We will forever be like Him!

So how can He not be ashamed of us when He sees us sin, fail and fall so miserably short? Because He sees us already made into the image of Christ. *He sees us done!*

However, for me to enjoy that freedom from shame and condemnation in this present struggle, I must humble myself, stop pretending and take full responsibility for my failure. I must learn to *"walk in the light"*.

Walk In The Light

When we take full blame, full responsibility for our sin, we can come before God without shame. The time for shame is not when we sin but when we refuse to take the blame for our sin. 1 John

1:7-10 says, *"...if we walk in the Light as He Himself is in the Light, we have fellowship with one another, and the blood of Jesus His Son cleanses us from all sin. If we say that we have no sin, we are deceiving ourselves and the truth is not in us. If we confess our sins, He is faithful and righteous to forgive us our sins and to cleanse us from all unrighteousness. If we say that we have not sinned, we make Him a liar and His word is not in us."* (NAS) The only place for shame here is if we say we have not sinned.

For many years I mistakenly thought *"walking in the light as He is in the light"* meant we were to learn to live without sin. Yet, it clearly cannot mean living in perfection, without sin, since one of the benefits of *"walking in the light"* is that the *"blood of Jesus keeps cleansing us of our sin"*. In fact, John warns us that if we pretend we don't sin then we lie. So, along with whatever other sin I am hiding in the dark, I can now add lying to my list of offenses.

To *"walk in the light"* is to keep nothing hidden, to expose through confession and to take the blame. This is the humility that gives us access to the true grace of God in our lives, now! Knowing Jesus died with all our shame, we can quickly take the blame knowing that we will be welcomed into the *Heavenly Doctor's* office for forgiveness and cleansing; for regenerating and renewing. When you know you can take the blame without the shame you will run to the doctor!

> *"Because of Christ and our faith in Him, we can now come fearlessly into God's presence, assured of his glad welcome."* (Eph 3:12 NLT)

There is no place here for shame. Because we believe Jesus took all our shame, we run fearlessly into the *Doctor's* office. We know He will welcome us gladly, examine us and fix us because that's what good doctors do. And the Great Physician is not just good...He's *great*!

The only place for shame before God is when I refuse to take the blame. When I say I am not sick, then the doctor cannot fix me. When I justify my sin, God cannot justify me. When I stubbornly refuse to confess my failure, I declare myself to be right...and God's judgment to be wrong. There is now shame because, in my unwillingness to confess, I am rejecting the sacrifice of Jesus so my shame remains alive.

No matter what ugly thing gets exposed in the clay, the Potter already knew it was hiding in there and He has been poking around so we will see it. Why? So He can remove it. The only reason the clay has to ever feel ashamed is if it refuses to be handled...*and gets off the wheel*. As we draw near to God, the Holy Spirit handles us and lovingly exposes what is hiding within us. We confess what is being exposed and He transforms us.

The best advice for the clay;

Stay on the wheel!

In order for me to cooperate with this process I must see it as positive and not negative. I must start seeing that it is good for me. I must not avoid it but embrace it. Enduring it when it is forced upon me by embarrassing exposure is not enough. I have to learn to love it and embrace it with joy, knowing the cleansing it will produce.

But to see it that way, I must have my mind renewed. Only then will I do a better job of *interacting with the Spirit* and regularly engaging with the ***True Transformer***.

213

Chapter Twenty-Two

Interact With
The True Transformer

We searchers want to be changed. We former *Promise Makers* crave a transformation that leaves us permanently different. We are tired of the temporary changes that occur when we get so mad at our failures that we are driven to crank up our will power one more time and make one more promise to God. We are looking for something beyond what our natural effort can produce; we are longing for supernatural transformation.

Most of us have experienced glimpses of it at times in our lives. Somewhere in our walk with God most of us have had a habit, an overwhelming temptation or a habitual way of thinking that held us captive. Then, one day we realized it was gone, changed; just not controlling us any longer. For some of us it was at our conversion, when we were first born again. For some it was after an unusual encounter with the Spirit or *"Spirit Baptism"*. For some, we just gradually realized we hadn't been compelled for a while and we didn't remember when the compulsion stopped. But we praised God for the change.

Most of us can't really explain how it happened, we just know it did. Like the formerly blind man Jesus healed and then left before the guy even knew who He was, our best explanation is; *"Once I was blind but now I see"*. It was there and it controlled me, and then it was gone. Though we will never be in control of the process, Jesus intends for that kind of on-going change to be a normal part of the Christian life.

Behavior Modification Or Transformation

The promise of modern psychology is limited behavior modification. The medical community generally holds that human personality is set as a combination of genetics and early childhood experiences; and can never be truly changed. But some enlightened people can become self-aware enough to modify their behavior and alter some of the results.

Behavior modification requires becoming aware of the thoughts and activities that are self-destructive or just don't give you the results you desire. Then you learn techniques to modify your thoughts and use your will power to change certain behaviors to reduce the self-destructive activities and increase the positive results you get from things or other people.

God has built into human creation a limited ability to modify and adapt. Human beings almost always modify or adapt based on selfish interests. The law of sowing and reaping or *"cause and effect"* is based on self-interest and it is not, in itself, bad. If a friend punches you in the nose for the way you treat them we usually (1) change the way we treat them, or (2) change friends, or (3) learn a martial art so we can punch back. Once we have been burned we usually modify the way we handle the stove. When given the choice of getting to work on time or being fired, we usually choose to get there on time. Well, some people do...sometimes. When given the choice of disobeying or being punished, children choose to obey. Well, sometimes...as long as there is a real risk of getting caught and the punishment is unpleasant enough. But frequently, they don't change even then.

My grandfather used to say *"Some people live and learn...but most just live"*. I'm afraid I am part of that last group far more than I want to admit. The old adage that *"Hindsight is 20/20"* just doesn't prove to be consistently true or we wouldn't make the same bad choice more than once...but we do.

It is generally held that human personality and core values do not change. Whatever changes do occur through will power and self effort are nearly always due to enlightened self-interest; how I can more effectively get what I want...and get it with the least amount of resistance from others? This is the core question that drives most behavioral change.

Behavior modification certainly has its benefits in our fallen world. It does help our everyday life when people control their behavior enough so we can *"all just get along"*. I can think of lots of people who ought to modify their behavior; for my benefit, if not for theirs. But modern science generally agrees; people do not truly change at their core being, they just modify and adapt as long as it directly benefits them.

But the promise of the Gospel is true change; true transformation. The hope of the *New Way* is that a power greater than ourselves will cause genuine heart change; which will result in positive personality change, which will result in lasting behavioral change...while we live in peace and joy through the ups and downs of this life-long process.

Wow, now that is a mouthful!

"Genuine heart change; which will result in positive personality change, which will result in lasting behavioral

change...while we live in peace and joy through the ups and downs of this life-long process."

The possibilities and ramifications of that statement are huge...HUGE! Yet this is the lifestyle the New Testament presents as the *"normal Christian life"*. We have been invited to join the Holy Spirit in this life-long process of on-going transformation, a life-long process of progressive sanctification. *"Once I was like that but now I am like this"* should be a regular testimony for the people who are living the *easy* and *light* life; former *"Promise Maker"* Club members like us who are now living the *New Way*.

However, the New Testament makes it clear that this type of life becomes a reality only to the extent that we –

1) **Believe** that His plan is to actually live through us;
2) **Humble ourselves** and stop pretending we can do it; and,
3) **Interact** with the *true transformer*, the Holy Spirit.

Conform Or Be Transformed

The amazing promise of Biblical grace is not behavior modification but true transformation. In fact, the Bible makes it clear that we must fight against *"conforming"* to the image of this world but we must passionately pursue *"being transformed"* by the work of the Spirit into the image of Christ. So before we examine the process, let me give you the punch line –

Conforming is something negative I do.
Transforming must be done to me!

The Scripture uses two different words to describe what we do (*conform*) and what the Spirit does to us (*transform*). 1 Peter 1:14 warns us to *"not be conformed to the former lusts which were yours in your ignorance"*. Paul says the same thing in Rom. 12:2, *"Do not be conformed to this world"*. In each of these verses, the word used for *"conform"* means to *"fashion yourself"*. It means to outwardly imitate or mold yourself to the behavior we see in the world. This is something we often do and it is destructive.

But the promise of true grace is that the Spirit will do something *to* us that will change the very essence of who and what we are. We don't stop conforming to the world because we decide to stop conforming, but because we are being changed at the very core of who we are. The Bible refers to this as *"transformation"*. The Greek word used for this *"transformation"* literally means *"**metamorphose**"*.

Tadpoles Into Frogs

Every grade school student comes to understand the process of *metamorphosis* by watching a tadpole change into a frog or seeing a caterpillar spin a cocoon and come out a butterfly. This is not behavior modification; this is *true transformation*.

Getting my dog to stay in the yard by shocking him every time he steps over an invisible line, now that's behavior modification. And it can save a dog's life. But a caterpillar into a butterfly? That is *true transformation*. The very essence and character of the being has been changed. It no longer looks the same; it no longer acts the same; it no longer *is* the same; it has been *transformed*. Some amazing chemical process which I cannot understand has been occurring *inside* that causes a complete change on the *outside.* This is metamorphosis; *change on the inside that, over time, shows up on the outside.*

Metamorphosis (*transformation*) is the promise of true grace; an on-going interaction between us and the Holy Spirit that causes miraculous change in the very essence of who we are, what we are, how we think and how we behave. There is instantaneous change; being born again of incorruptible seed, freely reconciled to God and made to be children of the Father. And there is progressive change; being increasingly sanctified and growing into the image of His Son. This progressive change is the miraculous process of *"spiritual tadpoles becoming Christ-like frogs"*.

We are given a very literal promise that our physical bodies will one day be *"glorified"*, changed from mortal to immortal as Christ's physical body was changed in the resurrection. *"...Christ, who will <u>transform</u> the body of our humble state into <u>conformity</u> with the body of His glory..."* (Phil 3:20-21 NAS). In this passage both words, *transform* and *conformity,* come from the same root word and convey the truth of metamorphosis; our bodies will be truly and forever changed by God's power transforming the very essence of what they are, into what they will be...for eternity. Paul sums up the transformation of our human bodies by saying, *"mortality will put on immortality"*.

We are also given the promise of *"metamorphose"* in our character and personality; here and now. Paul refers to this process in Rom. 12:2 – *"...do not be conformed to this world, but be transformed by the renewing of your mind..."* The word *"conformed"* used here means to *"fashion yourself"*. Unfortunately, that's what we tend to do. But the word *"transformed"* means *"to be changed, metamorphose"*. Again we see this truth –

Conforming is something negative I do.

Transforming is what the Holy Spirit does to me.

If we put this into modern computer language, we could say, *"Don't keep imitating the world but allow the Spirit to keep morphing you into Christ's image"*. Paul understood the *"morphing"* power of the Holy Spirit and knew it was the only way to experience true transformation.

But this process of spiritual metamorphose is *mysterious*; it's hard to explain and difficult for our minds to understand. It is much easier to learn a list of multiplication tables than it is to truly understand how a hairy, wiggling worm goes into a cocoon and comes out a beautiful, graceful butterfly. There is a miraculous, inexplicable process at work in there somewhere. It is much easier to tell someone to memorize a list of rules than to teach them how to interact with the *miraculous working of an invisible Spirit.*

Morphing Into Christ-Likeness

Paul traveled throughout Asia teaching people that the *New Way of the Spirit* was that God offered them the free gift of righteousness and that Christ would then live in and through them, progressively transforming them into His likeness. He was deeply grieved when he learned that some of his Gentile converts were later being taught that the way to become more Christ-like in their behavior was to use their will power to learn and keep all the Jewish rules instead of trusting and interacting with the Holy Spirit.

In Gal 4:21, Paul told them he felt like a woman in the labor of child birth until Christ was *"formed in you again"*. The Greek word Paul used for *"formed"* is another variation of *"metamorphose"*. Can you imagine how important this was to Paul? *"Like a woman in labor!"* He was deeply pained because they were trusting in human effort instead of engaging in the *transforming, morphing work of the Spirit*. It seemed that the more they learned the *"rules of righteousness"*, the less they depended on and interacted with the Spirit. Sound familiar to any of us *"Promise Makers"*?

The New Living Translation helps us here by quoting Paul as saying *"I feel as if I am going through labor pains for you again, and they will continue until Christ is fully developed in your lives"*. The *"development of Christ in our lives"* is a mysterious, progressive work of the Spirit that cannot be reduced to a set of written rules which human beings can grit their teeth and accomplish. This *"developing of Christ...Christ being formed in you"* is the miraculous work of the Spirit *in* us that reflects His nature *out* of us.

This process of Christ being *"formed within you"* or *"fully developed in your lives"* is not referring to salvation. These people were born again. They were saved by trusting in Christ's work on the cross. Paul was trying to bring them back to understanding that living the Christian life is not about learning rules and regulations but interacting with the Spirit who wants to live in and through us. And the development of His character within us depends on how much we *interact with His Spirit*.

But it is hard to explain something you can't see. Just as the caterpillar is being gradually changed under the cover of the cocoon, you and I are being transformed in our inner man under the cover of our outer body. You cannot see the changes the caterpillar is undergoing, but they are real. You cannot see the changes a grain of wheat goes through as it *"dies"* in the ground, but they are real. You cannot see the wind as it blows but the results of the wind can be seen; and they are real. And there are ways we can cooperate more effectively with the wind of the Spirit as He blows into our lives so we, and others, can see on the outside what has been changing on the inside.

Worship And Word – Focus And Feed

The part we play in this *metamorphose* is not complicated. The transforming power of the Spirit involves our interacting with Him through *worship* and the *word*. We present ourselves to Him in both; the various activities of *worship* and by meditating on the *word*. We set our minds on the Spirit both by communing with Him in *worship* and feeding on His *word*. The Scripture makes these two truths clear –

1) **We become more like what we *focus* on.** *(Worship)*
2) **What we *feed* will grow.** *(Word)*

Paul repeatedly tells us *"the mind set on the flesh produces death but the mind set on the Spirit produces life"* and to *"set our minds on things above"*. Paul tells us as we *"behold Him"* we are being changed into the same image we are looking at. James says as we look into *"the perfect law of liberty through life in the Spirit"* we are being changed into what we are looking at. Here we see this truth –

We become more like what we *focus* on.

The apostles tell us we must desire both the *milk* and the *meat* of the Word if we are to grow in grace. Jesus said we can only truly live this *easy* and *light* life if we eat *"every word that comes from God's mouth"*. Ezekiel was told to *"eat the words of the scroll"* and speak God's words to the people. David spoke about how sweet and nourishing the words of God were to his soul. Solomon said *"His words are sweeter than honeycomb, strength to our bones and nourishment to our hearts"*. Here we see this truth –

What we *feed* will grow.

These two truths work in the negative and the positive. For years I misunderstood God's nature and expectations so my adversary could keep me focusing and feeding on the wrong things. The result? I became more like what I was focusing on *(an angry God who demanded more than I could produce)* and what I fed kept growing *(fear, guilt, condemnation, frustration)*.

Now that we have gotten our foundation right, now that we have started at the right starting place, this process is really not complicated. It's not automatic and we have to fight for it, but it is not complicated. The Law is complicated, the rules and demands of the *Old Way* are complicated; the *New Way* of the perfect law of liberty in Christ is not.

Worship, in all its different forms of expression, is designed by God to enable us to *focus* on and interact with Him. The written *word* is design by God to help us *feed* on His truth and grow in His way of thinking. *Worship* involves our minds but it must become a *"spirit to spirit"* activity because, as spirit beings, transformation must be from the inside out; from our spirit to our outer man. Reading the written *word* must involve communing with the Spirit in worship because only He can cause the written word to become the *Living Word.* Learning the written word is only profitable when it drives us to encounter the *Living Word.*

We have spent the past twenty one chapters laying a firm foundation in the written Word so we are certain we are putting our *faith* in the right plan; and we are learning to *humble* ourselves quickly so we can access His grace. Now we must learn how to **interact** more effectively with the Spirit for the work of *transformation.*

Transformation *"To Do"* List

There are four passages I have found to be very helpful in showing me what I can do to *interact* with the Holy Spirit in a life-transforming way.

> *"Therefore I urge you, brethren, by the mercies of God, to present your bodies a living and holy sacrifice, acceptable to God, which is your spiritual service of worship. And do not be conformed to this world, but be <u>transformed by the renewing of your mind</u>, so that you may prove what the will of God is, that which is good and acceptable and perfect."* (Rom 12:1-2 NAS)

> *"But we all, with unveiled face, beholding as in a mirror the glory of the Lord, are <u>being transformed into the same image</u> from glory to glory, just as from the Lord, the Spirit."* (2 Cor. 3:18 NAS)

> *"Therefore let us <u>draw near</u> with confidence to the throne of grace, so that we may receive mercy and find grace to help in time of need."* (Heb 4:16 NAS)

> *"...<u>keep on being filled with the Spirit</u>, speaking to one another in psalms and hymns and spiritual songs, singing and making melody with your heart to the Lord; always giving thanks for all things in the name of our Lord Jesus Christ..."* (Eph. 5:18 NAS)

In these four passages we have an excellent *"transformation 'to do' list"*. But remember, these are not laws because laws don't give you the power to do them. However, laws do bring a punishment if you don't do them...perfectly! That is the failure of the *Old Way*.

Instead, these are *"commandments with promise"*; they promise that if we choose to agree with His ways, He will empower us to do the things we are agreeing with. And as we begin to do them, however imperfectly, we will experience a growing ability to do them more effectively. These *New Way* commandments tell us what we must do in order to get the benefits we want. But they also tell us we have the power of *"Christ in us"* to do them. And they give us the promise of what God will do in response.

Here is a simple list of things in these verses we must do and things He will do for us.

"Present your bodies in worship." I must do this.

"Be transformed by the renewing of your minds." He will do this.

"Behold His glory." I must do this.

"Be transformed into the same image." He will do this.

"Be changed by the Spirit." He will do this.

"Draw near in my time of need." I must do this.

226

"Draw near with confidence." I must do this.

"Receive mercy and find grace." He gives, I receive.

"Keep on being filled with the Spirit." *I do this...and He responds.*

"Keep making melody in your heart and giving thanks in everything!" *I must do this.*

Please Read This With *New Way* thinking

Though God has given me the power to do these things, I don't *have* to do them. I will not be punished if I don't do these things. But I won't get the benefits either. God will not stop loving me if I don't do these things. But I won't be able to enjoy His love. I will never come to truly know *"What God is really like"* and *"How He really feels about me"*. I will never be able to fully experience His life-transforming love; my *un-renewed mind* won't be able to comprehend it and my *weak spirit-man* won't able to receive it. My spiritual caterpillar will stay shriveled up in its cocoon wondering why the promise of its butterfly-experience doesn't *"just automatically happen"*.

And I will continue to wonder if there really is an *easy* and *light* life out there somewhere; and if there is, *why can't I find it and learn to live in it?*

It is this kind of thinking inside my head that must change.

But I need help.

I think I need to have my thought process re-wired!

Chapter Twenty-Three

Rewire The Way I Think

I act the way I act because I think the way I think.
Ways of thinking result in ways of behaving.
Attitudes produce actions.

Any lasting change in behavior, any true transformation from the inside out, must involve a renewing of our minds; a miraculous change in the way we think. This is why Paul wrote statements such as –

> *"Let this <u>mind</u> be in you that was in Christ Jesus."* (Phil. 2:5)
> *"The <u>mind</u> set on the Spirit produces life."* (Rom. 8:6)
> *"Be renewed in the spirit of your <u>mind</u>."* (Eph 4:23)

And one of the greatest promises for us who are searching for the *New Way of the Spirit* –

> *"...be transformed by the renewing of your mind..."* (Rom. 12:2)

The Greek word Paul uses for *"be transformed"* is the same word we have been dissecting throughout the last chapter – *"metamorphose"*. The transformation or *metamorphosis* that must happen to us comes as a result of having our minds renewed. The renewing of our minds can best be understood as *"re-wiring the way we think"* or *"re-wiring the way our thoughts are processed"*.

This *re-wiring* happens as the Holy Spirit turns the Written Word into the Living Word in our inner man. This miraculous and inexplicable process happens as we worship Him, meditate upon Him, commune with Him, focus on Him, behold His beauty, look upon His majesty, contemplate His goodness, be filled with Him; all the different ways the written Word tells us we can engage and interact with Him. This activity is spirit-to-spirit and heart-to-heart but the physical body plays a critical part.

Do Your Part – Present Your Body

Look at the larger passage –

> *"Therefore I urge you, brethren, by the mercies of God, to present your bodies a living and holy sacrifice, acceptable to God, which is your spiritual service of worship. And do not be conformed to this world, but be transformed by the renewing of your mind, so that you may prove what the will of God is, that which is good and acceptable and perfect."* (Rom 12:1-2 NAS)

Though this *"morphing"* process is mysterious and impossible to truly explain, the part we play is simple –

"Present your bodies…

in the service of worship…

and you will be transformed…

as your mind is being renewed!"

1) Present Your Bodies

The Greek word Paul used here for *"bodies"* is a word that means exactly that – *bodies*; mortal, physical, flesh and blood bodies. The *act* of worship means we must involve our bodies. Just thinking nice thoughts about God is fine...but it is not nearly enough. The act of presenting our bodies is part of the *medicine* we are responsible to take.

The Bible describes a wide variety of physical actions that God intends to be associated with worship; standing, kneeling, laying down, falling down, bowing down, jumping, hopping, dancing, raising hands, waving arms, speaking with our lips, singing, clapping, shouting, laughing for joy, waiting quietly in expectant silent contemplation; the Biblical list goes on and on, and all these actions are correct under the right circumstances. This is not intended to be a discussion about the differences in the way the Bible defines praise and worship or the protocol for each. The bottom line for our search is this: we must present our bodies for our minds and hearts to truly be involved.

2) The Activities of Worship

Worship must be a *verb* more than a noun. We must <u>*do*</u> worship! Yes, I know, singing is not, by itself, worship: clapping hands is not, by itself, worship. But God has created us so that the activities of our bodies in acts of worship give us the most effective way for our hearts and minds to become involved. We read and meditate on the Word with our minds but our bodies *do* worship! From the activity of the invisible God coming into the garden in some understandable form to fellowship Adam and Eve, all the way to the book of Revelation where we see every living thing lifting their voices in thunderous praise to Him who sits upon the throne, we see the bottom line; *worship involves bodily action!*

231

So we have Paul's commandment –

"Present your physical bodies in the activity of worship!"

The scriptures tell us that the spirit, soul and body of man are so intertwined that only the Holy Spirit can divide and deal with each of them (Heb. 4:12). So we are commanded to present our bodies in the activities of worship. Just the act of *doing something* focuses the mind and emotions in the right direction. *So we take our medicine by presenting our bodies in the actions of worship!*

3) Be Transformed

Only the Spirit can transform us, but we must learn to cooperate with Him in this activity; we must take our *medicine*. The Bible is filled with word-pictures to help us understand how to cooperate with the mysterious work of the Holy Spirit. Think about the pictures that come to mind when you read Biblical descriptions of how the Spirit interacted with people.

They were all filled; the Spirit was poured out; He came upon them; He fell upon them; the Spirit hovered over the deep; rest under the shadow of His wing; a cloud filled the Temple; the Spirit came like a dove; He is a cleansing fire; having our conscience washed; cleansing by the water of the word; a river will come from deep within you, a river flowed from the throne; etc.

I am sure you can think of many more Biblical word-pictures; some are quiet and calm, many are loud and enthusiastic. Both Old and New Testament people got pretty *"worked up"* in the activities of worship at times. The word-pictures God used in Scripture are to communicate to us concepts that are beyond our natural understanding. But the pictures give us clues as to how we can

232

cooperate with the Spirit; how we can *act* and *interact* with Him, how we can *take our medicine*. Most of these word-pictures have certain things in common.

- Most of these things are deliberate actions; they don't just automatically happen.

- They do require us to do something; they are not *"sovereign"* or automatic.

- They take time; you fill something gradually, shadows and clouds move slowly.

- This is a process; pouring out and filling up are each progressive activities.

- Each activity involves a surrendering of control and trusting Him.

- Each activity includes something we must expect the Spirit to do as we worship.

4) Your Mind is Re-wired

We are promised that, as we present our bodies in the activities of worship, the Spirit will do His work of *re-wiring our minds*. The Spirit reprograms the paths our thoughts travel. When we are faced with the same set of circumstances again, we are able to see things differently and we are empowered to choose a different reaction; a righteous response in place of our former carnal reaction. The divine nature begins to emerge, the mind of Christ begins to operate and the fruit of the Spirit begins to grow.

And when we fail, we quickly humble ourselves and take full responsibility for trusting in ourselves and we confess it as sin. We know He is not angry with us so we run to Him, presenting our bodies in worship and trusting Him to do more work on our minds, renewing and re-wiring how we think. This is the normal Christian life!

As we present our bodies in worship we must put our faith in the right place. We deny our faith in our ability by humbling ourselves, but we release our faith in His ability as we worship and expect Him to change us. We are never in control of *when, where* and *how* He does His work, but we are to expect Him to be faithful to His promise of *metamorphosis*!

Focus On Him And Be Transformed

Paul describes this process of worship and transformation in 2 Cor 3:18 –

> *"But we all, with unveiled face, beholding as in a mirror the glory of the Lord, are being transformed into the same image from glory to glory, just as from the Lord, the Spirit."* (NAS)

This is an amazing description of what we must expect to happen whenever we draw near to Him and present our bodies in worship. Once again, we see that the part we play is simple in action but mind-blowing in its possibilities –

We focus on Him in worship...

He transforms us...

We begin to look like what we are focusing upon...

This transformation is done by the power of the Spirit.

As we behold the Lord in our worship there is a transforming that we should expect to take place. Paul describes it with another word-picture. As we focus on Him it is like the reflection of a mirror. It's not actually a mirror but it's like one. This is the word-picture he wants us to envision so we know how to cooperate with Him. As we worship Him, moving our focus from our inability to His perfect ability, a transformation begins; *metamorphosis* progresses. The One we are beholding reflects into us. His image grows within us and begins to reflect out of us.

We begin to look like what we are looking at!

Similar to the way the life of God grew within Mary as the Spirit came upon her and *"overshadowed"* her, the image of Christ grows within us overtaking and *"morphing"* our image. Remember, the angel told Mary that the life of God was going to grow within her until it finally came out of her as the Son. Her only question was *"How can this happen with me since I am a virgin?"* Mary understood how women got pregnant and she knew that as a virgin she was missing an important part of the equation. The angel's answer was, *"The Holy Spirit will come upon you and the power of God will overshadow you"* (Luke 1:34). In other words, *"The Spirit is going to hover over you and put in you what you are lacking"*.

We frustrated *"Promise Makers"* know a similar feeling of lack. We want the life of Christ to grow within us and come through us, but we know we lack an important part of the equation. The answer? *Behold Him in worship* and the Spirit will keep transforming us, putting in us what we lack. Christ is being *formed in us* as we interact with the Spirit and let Him *hover* over us in worship. His life is being developed within us as we *focus our affection* upon Him in worship. *As we behold Him*, the written word is becoming the Living Word inside of us!

Don't Be In A Hurry

We must learn from the word-pictures in the Scriptures and not be in a hurry in our worship. Clouds and shadows tend to move slowly. Filling an empty glass is a gradual process and takes time. Metamorphosis takes time and much of it goes on unseen. In our passage, 2 Cor. 3:18, Paul describes this progressive process happening from *"glory to glory"*. The word he uses here for *"glory"* literally means *"to reveal, to manifest or to show clearly"*.

God is omnipresent. He is everywhere at all times. Yet, throughout the Bible God has chosen to *"draw near, manifest, show Himself and reveal Himself"* to people who seek Him. James' instruction to *"draw near to God and He will draw to you"* is not just some reassuring platitude. God means it. He wants to reveal Himself to us in ways we can know and feel. God clearly delights in breaking through the *barrier of divine invisibility* and encountering us in ways we can sense. These are the encounters where transformation takes place. Though we can never demand the *manner* in which He will reveal Himself, the Bible is filled with overwhelming evidence that the Almighty God wants to reveal Himself to us. He truly wants us to encounter Him!

Since the word *"glory"* means *"reveal* or *"manifest"*, *"from glory to glory"* can be understood as *"from revelation to revelation"* or *"from encounter to encounter"* or *"from manifestation to manifestation"*. Every time we sense His presence, every time we see something new about Him, every time we understand something a bit differently or see a truth more clearly; we are affected, we are being changed.

Each time we encounter Him in any way something inside of us changes. Through meditating on the written Word, prayer and passionate worship we encounter Him and our thoughts are being rearranged, our thinking is being re-wired. More of His nature and character is revealed to us; more of His Spirit fills us. As we more frequently and more wholeheartedly draw near to Him, He will draw near to us. And transformation takes place. Change occurs. *"From encounter to encounter"* we are being transformed. Transformation is being done *to* us. This is the *"Do-It-To-Me"* Solution! *Jehovah M'kadesh* keeps revealing Himself to us and from revelation to revelation we keep reflecting more of His image.

Enter In And Enjoy His Love

I fall short of my expectations in many ways. But one thing I have learned is how to regularly enter into, and enjoy, the presence of God. I do regularly encounter God. I can't always encounter Him exactly when I want or exactly how I would like; and I certainly can't get Him to do all the things I would prefer He do at the time I would prefer He do them...but I am regularly able to truly enter in and deeply enjoy His presence.

It's certainly not because I am so special or so wonderful, but it is because I have learned something important about the role of the Holy Spirit. One of the primary jobs of the Spirit is to *"pour the love of God"* into the hearts of people who draw near to Him. I have come to expect Him to do that job on a regular basis, and I position myself through worship so He can regularly pour the Father's love into me.

Paul tells us the most important foundation we must have for our lives is to be rooted and grounded in the revelation of God's unconditional love for us.

> *"May your roots go down deep into the soil of God's marvelous love. And may you have the power to understand, as all God's people should, how wide, how long, how high, and how deep His love really is."* (Eph. 3:17-19 NLT)

Paul makes it clear that it is absolutely critical for us to grow in our understanding of *how wide, how long, how high, and how deep* the love of God is for us.

Think about Paul's description of God's love. *"How wide, how long, how high, how deep"*. This is a man who is passionately in love with God and believes the Almighty God is passionately in love with him! This is a former Pharisee who has moved way beyond some clinical, theological, sterile definition of the love of God. Paul is a man who is *"head-over-heels"* in love with God and he is convinced the heavenly Father is *"head-over-heels"* in love with him. This is a man who really believes he is part of the bride who is enraptured with the love of her bridegroom. This is truly a man who has learned how to *enter into* and *truly enjoy* the love of God.

Now focus on the work of the Holy Spirit as He longs to *"pour the love of God into your heart"*. This is not some well-ordered church service, some somber traditional observance. This is deep, passionate, enveloping, liquid love from God being poured into your heart; soaking, marinating and tenderizing our hearts, giving us a peace and joy that is not dependent on the current circumstances of life. This is the kind of experience God wants each of us to have with the Spirit on a regular basis.

I must say that again; *soaking, marinating and tenderizing our hearts, giving us a peace and joy that is not dependent on the current circumstances of life.* (Selah…chew on that for a while!)

Paul tells us this revelation must come from encountering the Holy Spirit who will enable us to *"know the love of Christ which surpasses knowledge!"* Think of it. A *"knowing"* that surpasses knowledge; a revelation that doesn't come from *"book-learning"* but as direct input from the Spirit into our hearts. This can only be experienced as we encounter the Spirit by communing with Him through deep, heart-revealing, thought-rewiring worship. The written Word tells us what we lack and what we should ask for, and that is essential. But this revelation only comes through communing and encountering Him by His Spirit. This is where He *"pours the love of God into our hearts"* (Rom. 5:5).

Notice, He doesn't pour the love of God into our minds but into our hearts. This revelation of unconditional love is not something we reason out with our minds but something He communicates *"spirit to spirit"*, *"heart to heart"*. And our hearts will tell our minds what to think. When the Spirit *"roots and grounds us in His love"* we have a strength that is not our own. Circumstances don't dictate to a heart that is rooted and grounded in His love. *Unwavering peace* and *abounding joy* grow in a heart that is rooted and grounded in His unconditional love.

The Spirit Worships From Within Us

Paul says the Spirit wants to empower us to worship from our deepest being by actually worshipping God *through* us.

> *"Because you are sons, God has sent forth the Spirit of His Son into our hearts, crying, 'Abba! Father!'."* (Gal 4:6-7 NAS)

The Father sends His Spirit into our hearts to worship through us. The Holy Spirit longs to empower our ability to engage in deep, passionate worship by crying out inside of us back to the Father, *"My dear Father!"* Imagine what it would be like to get in tune with the Holy Spirit within us as He is crying out His perfect love for the Father...*through us!*

> *"...you have received a spirit of adoption as sons by which we cry out, "Abba! Father!"* (Rom 8:15 NAS)

Now we cry out, *"Abba Father!"* The *spirit of adoption* is poured into our hearts and we begin to cry out to the Father as the Spirit is crying out through us.

See the process –

1) The Spirit pours the unconditional love of God into our hearts. He then begins to worship the Father through us by crying out *"My dear Father!"* As we turn our attention from our inability and focus on His magnificent promises, we begin to sense something inside of us crying out to the Father. It is Him, the Holy Spirit, worshipping the Father through us!

2) We begin to cooperate by presenting our bodies in deep, passionate worship and allowing this cry rising up within us to come out in our voice. We begin to cry out, empowered by the Spirit within us, *"My dear Father!"*

3) As we interact through worship, the Spirit pours more of the love of God into our hearts and we grow in our comprehension of just how wide, how long, how deep and how high His love for us really is...*and nothing can shake the foundation that is being built!*

I have learned the hard way that all of this will be short-circuited if we don't know what to do when we fail. And we will fail. So we better get God's perspective on our failures or our adversary will beat us every time.

So what should we do when we blow it?

Chapter Twenty-Four

Tying Up Loose Ends

We have come a long way in our search for the *New Way*, the *easy* and *light* life Jesus promised. Hopefully, we have learned that this is a journey and not a destination. We will be continually learning and re-learning as we stay in the yoke with Jesus and spend the rest of our lives *"learning of Him and His ways"*. But before we go off on our own more individual journeys, we need to tie up some loose ends, address some final questions, and distill all this down to a few simple steps.

Remember, those early disciples didn't have any of the study aides we have. They didn't have bibles, teaching CDs, instructional DVDs, commentaries, translations; they couldn't even run to Wal-mart and get note-taking materials. They could talk to each other, listen to the teachers and interact with the Spirit. That's about it. So this had to be simple and easy to remember.

I have an entire library of study aides on my computer. I have several translations with a Strong's concordance just on my phone! I love study aides. But I see that I am just beginning to learn how to interact and depend on the Spirit the way those early believers did. Paul's warning certainly applies to us modern seekers – *"I fear...that your minds will be led astray from the simplicity and purity of devotion to Christ."* (2 Cor. 11:3 NAS) Remember, the

Law is complicated on purpose; so we will give up and run to Christ. The New Way of life in the Spirit is simple; learn to let Him live through us and trust that He knows what He is doing.

Let's address a few questions before we wrap all this up.

What should I do when I fail?

James said, *"We all stumble in many ways"* (James 3:2). John said, *"If we say we do not sin, we lie"* (1 John 1:8-10). Paul said *"I have not attained to all I am teaching you nor have I become perfect"* (Phil. 3:12). Each of these men understood how to deal with their failure without excusing it or being overcome with condemnation. They each understood what to do when they failed – *draw near to God!*

> *"Therefore, let us draw near with confidence to the throne of grace, so that we may receive mercy and find grace to help in time of need."* (Heb 4:16 NAS)

The verse just before this one tells us we have *"a High Priest who understands our weaknesses"*. The word *"therefore"* lets us know that the *"time of need"* referred to in the above passage is whenever our weaknesses show up and we fail to act Christ-like. We can better understand this passage by reading it like this –

- *Because our High priest understands our weaknesses...*

- *In our time of need, when a weakness shows its ugly head...*

- *Draw near with confidence...*

- *Come to the throne of God's unearned life-changing power...*

- *Receive His mercy...*

- ***Expect to be empowered by His grace!***

When we fail, when we fall short, when we give into our weakness, when our *"flesh flops out for all to see,"* that is when we must draw near to His throne to receive His mercy and grace to help us. This is the most critical time to interact with the Holy Spirit; when we have fallen short. It is also when we experience the greatest pressure to *draw back* in shame.

Notice the difference between *mercy (God's unconditional love)* and *grace (The unearned power of Christ living through us).* We need them both. When you fail, you need His mercy to wash you in His unconditional love. But you need His grace to empower you to change. When you have done all you can do to get well, don't be ashamed to go to the Heavenly Doctor and get your medicine. Shame is the trick of your adversary to keep you from the help you need. His plan is to get us to draw back. The Holy Spirit invites us to draw near...in our failure!

Amazingly, this verse says we are to come to His throne with confidence when we have failed. *Confidence?! When we fail?! When our weakness gets exposed?!* This goes against all human logic.

We walk slowly by the principal's office right after we aced the test, not when we failed miserably. We strut by the coach's office after we made the play that won the game, not after we struck out four times in a row. We stop by to see the boss right after we made the sale that will bring huge profit to the company's bottom line, not after we overslept and missed out on the sale of the year.

But God's loving *Brilliant Plan* for us is just the opposite. He wants us to draw near to Him quickly when we fail so He can wash us, empower us and remind us once again that it's not by our power, not by our might, but by His Spirit at work in us. So get to the heavenly doctor as quickly as you can and take all your medicine!

When will I become perfectly like Christ?

The Bible is clear that Christ-like, sinless perfection will only be achieved when we appear before God and the metamorphosis is completed; when He makes us forever like His Son. *"Beloved, now we are children of God, and it has not appeared as yet what we will be. We know that when He appears, we will be like Him, because we will see Him just as He is."* (1 John 3:2 NAS)

This complete transformation will happen to all who follow Him because He has predestined it. *"For those whom He foreknew, He also predestined to become conformed to the image of His Son."* (Rom 8:29)

Sinless perfection is not a destination we will arrive at in this life. Any who claim they have arrived at sinless perfection have grossly underestimated the fullness of Christ's perfect nature and have justified their watered-down definition of sin. They have also set a standard that even God does not expect. We are pilgrims on the journey with Him, learning His ways until He calls us home to Himself. We will be rewarded in His eternal Kingdom for our progress in this life. But when we stand before Him, He will complete the work of *metamorphose* and we will all be *made* like Him, forever. And He will get all the credit, for all eternity!

How do I know if I am trusting the true grace of God?

James makes it clear that if we are trusting the grace of God then we will see good works growing in our lives; not perfected but growing. He tells us that if we say we have this *New Way* faith then it should be evident by the works it produces. Those works are the fruit of the Spirit and the many different ways they show through our behavior. But those good works also include how quickly we confess and take full responsibility for where we still fall short. 1 John 1:9, *"If we confess our sins He is faithful and just to forgive our sins and cleanse us from all unrighteousness,"* is a commandment we are to obey when we have failed to obey other commandments. When we confess our failure to obey, we are obeying!

By looking at the Biblical models of Paul, Peter, James, John, and all the other examples, it is clear that the normal Christian life sometimes *appears* to be *"three steps forward and two steps back"*. In fact, it sometimes *feels* like *"two steps forward and three steps back"*! But this pattern of life is normal and it is clearly born out in the Scriptures.

Peter's sin of denying Christ the night He was arrested was directly due to his fear of what those people would do to him. Yet, about fifty days later on the day of Pentecost, Peter had no fear of getting up and speaking directly, and harshly, to the same leaders who crucified the Lord. The Holy Spirit had changed him. But a few years later, Paul writes that he had to *"confront Peter to his face"* (Gal. 2:11) because of the hypocritical way he treated the Gentile believers out of fear of what the Jewish believers might think of him. Clearly, Peter had gone *"three giant steps forward"* at Pentecost and at least a step or two back later on. Paul certainly thought he had gone back a couple of steps. We don't know if Peter ever got completely free from his fear of what others might think of him. But we can be assured, the moment he appeared before the Throne after his death, he got completely free from that fear because he was instantly made forever like Jesus!

Hebrews 11 lists people who did great things by faith. Yet, the Spirit inspired the biblical writers to record the huge mistakes and blatant disobedience of nearly all of them. But at the end of their lives it is clear God had a different perspective of their hearts than we might have.

We must keep assuring our hearts that we have a High Priest who understands our weaknesses and keep drawing near to Him when we fail! This passage is worthy of needle pointing on a pillow…or tattooing on your arm:

> *"Because of Christ and our faith in Him, we can now come fearlessly into God's presence, assured of his glad welcome."* (Eph. 3:12 NLT)

Tell me one more time, what are the 3 things I am supposed to do?

Faith, humility, and interaction with the Spirit!

1) Choose to put your *faith*, at all times, in God's *Brilliant Plan*; *Christ living in and through you!*

2) Quickly *humble* yourself by confessing your failure, without excuse, and deny your ability to make yourself like Christ.

3) *Interact* with the Holy Spirit by drawing near to God to receive both His mercy and the power of His grace.

This is the *standard operating procedure* I am pursuing for my life.

- I choose to deny my ability to truly change myself.
- I choose to declare my confidence that I am unconditionally loved by God and that His grace, *Christ in me*, is sufficient to change me.

- I choose to humble myself by quickly confessing my sin and taking full responsibility for my failure...without condemnation.

- I choose to interact with the Spirit by worshipping His majesty, giving thanks for His unwavering goodness toward me and regularly being filled with the Spirit.

- I choose to feed myself on the Word in a way that builds me up and increases my confidence that *"He who began this work in me, He will complete it"*.

And, though not anywhere near perfectly, I am, with increasing consistency, experiencing *unwavering peace* and *abounding joy*!

To all my former fellow *"Promise Makers"*, I encourage you on your journey into the *easy* and *light* life, with this:

When things go well, draw near to God.

When you fail miserably, draw near to God.

In all things, in all circumstances, in all situations...

draw near to God.

We can be assured of His glad welcome!

You know, that might be a good idea for a book.

And now it is!

Continue your journey by getting Mark's next book at markdrakeministries.com

God's Brilliant Plan has now gone around the world and is being used on five continents to train leaders how to teach people to live in radical, transforming Grace and the true New Covenant.

You can now order a variety of resources to help get these important truths deep into your heart and mind.

God's Brilliant Plan Study Guide- $15.00

-The Companion Study Guide takes you through the book, page by page, paragraph by paragraph, asking you questions and helping you incorporate the answers into your daily life.

God's Brilliant Plan Seminar-

-Mark brought together forty leaders and taught through the book, chapter by chapter, for 10 hours over two days. The seminar is presented in 8 sessions on DVD or Audio CD.

Complete Seminar on 5 DVDs- $60.00
Complete Seminar on 8 Audio CDs- $40.00

God's Brilliant Plan Audio Book- $30.00

-The complete unabridged book read by Mark on 8 audio CDs.

Visit us at
www.markdrakeministries.com